THETFORD
A CENTURY REMEMBERED

CW01662804

TO THE INHABITANTS OF THE

BOROUGH of THETFORD.

HIS ROYAL HIGHNESS

THE

PRINCE OF WALES

Will pass through the Borough on Monday afternoon, December 9th, 1901, *en-route* to Elveden Hall, and as it is His first visit since His accession to the title, I shall be very pleased if the inhabitants will decorate and illuminate their houses for the occasion (more especially those in Station Road, White Hart Street, Bridge Street, and London Road), and allow the decorations to remain till Friday, December 13th, on which day His Royal Highness will return.

WALTER C. FISON,

Ford Place, **MAYOR.**

Thetford,

December 2nd, 1901.

H. Green, Machine Printer, Thetford.

THETFORD
A CENTURY REMEMBERED

From 1900
to the Present Day

David Osborne

"Visions of Thetford shall remain,
Thetford shall still our hearts retain,
In bonds of loyalty".

From the School Song of Thetford Grammar School, 'The Song of Thetford', verse 2

Published
by
D. Osborne
1996

Published
by
David Osborne

British Library Cataloguing in Publication Data
Osborne, David
Thetford - A Century Remembered
ISBN - 0 9513484 1 8
Typeset and Printed by Geo. Reeve Ltd.,
Town Green, Wymondham, Norfolk
First Published 1996
© D. J. Osborne, 1996

All rights reserved. No part of this publication may be reproduced, stored in a retrieval system, or transmitted in any form or by any means electronic, mechanical, photocopying, recording or otherwise, without the prior written permission of the copyright owner.

Front cover:
REMINISCING BY THE MARKET PLACE, 1956
Left-right: Mr William Leonard, aged 86 years; Mr Henry Bassingthwaite, aged 80 years;
Mr Charles Lane, aged 65 years; Mr Fred Gooch, aged 83 years and Mr Joseph French, aged 76 years.
[Photograph courtesy of Eastern Counties Newspapers]

Back cover: **TOWN BRIDGE, c.1905 & 1996**

Inside plate: **THETFORD FROM THE AIR, 1981**
[Photograph by Derek A. Edwards (courtesy of Norfolk Museum Services), 30 June 1981.
Ref:TL8683/T/AQT25]

ACKNOWLEDGEMENTS

I wish to thank the many individuals and organisations without whose help this book would not have been possible.

For the loan of photographs: Constance M. Beckett, Gladys Blackburn, Pat Boughen, Brian Boughton, Peter Bowes, Marcus Bunning, Judy & Garry Burrell, Michael Burton, Brian Carr, Rita Christian, Alan Clarke, Mary Clarke, J. A. Clark & Co., Violet Clarke, Dominic Cragoe, Jennifer Elvidge, Ann Fuller, Cecil Germany, Mary Hayes, Nessie Horwood, Norma Howard, Geoff Howlett, Eric Hubbard, Audrey Humphrey, Percy James, Denise Jones, Joyce Jones, Daisy Kenny, John 'Charlie' Leeder, May & Bill Leeder, Arthur Lockwood, Florrie Lockwood, Evelyn Ollington, Audrey Osborne, Eric Pilbrow, Richard Potter, Eileen Roberts, Wendy Serjeant, Peter Starling, Bob Thompson, 'Ted' Trumpess, and Geoff 'Hippy' Wright.

For the various individuals and organisations who have allowed me to publish photographs from their collections: Ancient House Museum, Thetford; Barry Griggs; Bristol Vintage Bus Group; Bury Free Press; Carl Richards; Charles Burrell Museum, Thetford; East Anglian Film Archive; Eastern Counties Newspapers; Hunting Aerofilms Ltd; Imperial War Museum, London; John C. Baker; J. Sainsbury, Thetford; Norfolk Air Photographs Library, Gressenhall; Studio Five, Thetford; Thetford Dolphins ASC; Thetford Rugby Club; Thetford Town Council.

My grateful thanks are also extended to exiled Thetfordian, Brian Carr, for his editorial contribution and comments, Eastern Counties Newspapers for allowing me access to the Thetford & Watton Times 1959-1980 an invaluable source of information. My thanks also to Michael Carnell, Chief Librarian at the County Library, Thetford, and Oliver Bone, Curator of the Ancient House Museum, for allowing me access to archive material in their custody. I should also like to acknowledge the enthusiastic help given by Derek Edwards, Air Photography Officer, Norfolk Museums Service.

Photographs not acknowledged are from the David Osborne collection.

INDEX
[Bold numerals denote photograph]

Continued on page 130

FOREWORD

by Mr Charles W. Brown.

Born at Thetford in 1898, Charles W. Brown is one of Thetford's oldest residents and has spent many years serving the community as a J.P., Chairman of Thetford Town F.C., President of Thetford & District Historical Society, Superintendent of the Methodist Sunday Schools and President of Thetford Natural History Society.

I congratulate Mr David Osborne on the publication of what I am sure will be a very successful book.

Having known and lived in Thetford for most of this century, it holds a very special place in my heart - and my own life is tied-up with its development, as indeed have the lives of several generations of my family.

As a boy, I well remember the great attraction that the water meadows held for me, I spent many happy hours on the river. The town has always been greatly blessed by the natural beauty within it and surrounding it - beauty I have appreciated so much.

A significant part of my working life was spent at the Burrell's Works, learning my trade as a metal turner and helping to produce the road rollers and traction engines that provided the industrial lifeblood for the town in the early part of the century.

In recent years, of course, the town has grown and developed to an enormous extent and I am pleased that so much of its history will be preserved through the medium of the photographs in this book.

I trust that all who look through its pages will gain an insight into the unique character and charm that is Thetford and that its modern-day citizens will be enriched by this glimpse of its past as the town moves forward into a new century.

Charles W. Brown, Thetford, 1996

CONTENTS

THETFORD'S POPULATION

1801 - 2,246
1851 - 4,074
1891 - 4,322
1901 - 4,613
1911 - 4,778
1921 - 4,705
1931 - 4,098
1941 - No Census
1951 - 4,447
1961 - 5,398
1971 - 13,706
1981 - 19,593
1991 - 19,901

INTRODUCTION

'How thoughtless it would be if we allowed that part of history that is closest, to just pass us by'.

T**hetford - A Century Remembered'** is a photographic record of Twentieth Century Thetford. With the century rapidly drawing to a close, it is an appropriate time to reflect and look back on the last ninety years or so - an era marked by considerable progress, social change and incident.

There can be few alive today whose personal memories reach back to the first decade of the twentieth century when Thetfordians shared a different life-style and values, in many ways, so different and remote from our own. In those early days, Thetford was best known as an ancient borough and for the manufacture of traction engines and pulp-ware.

Although progress was gradually changing things with new ideas, fashions and inventions, something of Victorian and Edwardian life could still be found into the middle of 20th century Thetford. In some ways Thetford and its inhabitants, as indeed did other parts of Norfolk, continued to lag behind the latest innovations. Nonetheless, from being a place somehow 'behind the times' and enveloped in a kind of stagnation, local life during the last four decades has seen profound changes. The old town centre has virtually been rebuilt and where fields and countryside once surrounded the town, large housing and industrial estates have been constructed to accommodate both new settlers and the indigenous population. Moreover, besides this easily recognisable transformation, there is hardly a sphere of local life that has not been touched by progress. Indeed we Thetfordians of the twentieth century have experienced what must be one of the most significant periods of the town's history, a past that reaches back over one thousand years.

Even though there is much that has been forgotten, our individual memories of Thetford and the twentieth century will undoubtedly cover an enormous range of experiences, incidents and people, from every-day life to more profound events. The two world wars and the upheaval they caused ought to be vividly remembered, along with the inevitable changes that such conflicts created. Afterwards life was never to be quite the same, if indeed it ever has been from year to year.

Thetford was certainly a different place after the 1914-18 War when it suffered one of its worst periods of industrial and economic depression. Once thriving industries and businesses closed and people drifted away from the town, looking for work and opportunities elsewhere.

Between 1939-45, local life was again disrupted and turned upside down by world conflict. Once more, Thetfordians were deeply involved in the war effort and the security of town and nation. Thetford came to be known to thousands of allied soldiers and airmen from all over the world, as they passed through the town at some stage during the war.

After peace was declared and some kind of normality returned, people expected a better future. It was probably this optimism that prompted Thetford Borough Council to make the momentous and historic decision in the 1950s to develop and create the town we know today. Many of you who left London and settled in Thetford as a result of this decision, will remember leaving the familiar surroundings of a large city and your first impressions of the town and surrounding Breckland.

Born in 1948, my personal memories go back no further than the early 1950s. I can clearly recall walking round the numerous building sites in the late 1950s and early 60s, watching with interest and excitement the construction of the new Thetford. But neither can I forget the old buildings and shops that existed before the redevelopment of the town centre, nor one of my earliest memories of a public event, standing with other children on the Market Place in 1953, waiting to receive a Coronation goblet from the Mayor.

You will all have your own memories. No doubt many of you will be able to recall events and scenes that deserve recognition but have gone unmentioned in this publication. For this I apologise, for even with the benefit of photography and well-documented evidence, it is not practically possible to describe all that ought to be remembered of twentieth century Thetford - if only it were. Nonetheless, throughout this book I have endeavoured to include some of the most fascinating and important aspects of local life. I have also aimed to strike a balance between the different periods and chosen subjects. To some extent I have been guided by the legacy of photographs.

One of the many advantages we have over our ancestors is that, for the very first time, it has been possible to illustrate with photographs a whole century of life and all it embraces, even though few people in the town owned a camera in the early years of the century. I hope that the illustrations and accompanying text, recording something of the countless and immeasurable changes to twentieth century life, will provide a valuable impression and help to preserve your memories as we enter a new millennium.

David Osborne, Thetford 1996

ROYAL VISITS
&
CORONATIONS

'This place hath been honoured with the presence of many Kings and Queens, several of which used to reside here for some time together'. Francis Blomfield, 'The Burgh of Thetford', published 1739

VISIT OF KING EDWARD VII, December, 1903

The 20th century was only a few hours old before the bells of St Peter's Church were ringing to welcome HRH the Prince of Wales, *en route* to Elveden Hall as a guest of the Earl of Iveagh.

Just one year later, on the 22nd January 1901, the bells of St Peter's Church tolled the death of Queen Victoria who had died in the evening of the previous day. After such a long reign, the news *'The Queen is dead'* seemed so unreal. Flags flew at half-mast over the town, as Thetford joined the nation in mourning.

In this view, Queen Victoria's successor, King Edward VII inspects the local Volunteer Battalion at the railway station on his return to Sandringham, after one of his frequent shooting holidays at Elveden.

CORONATION AVENUE, c.1910

The coronation of King Edward VII took place in August 1902. Coloured bunting and flags decorated the streets and buildings of the town. A band played on the Market Place, and in a field near the Melford Bridge a carnival, sports and a fireworks display completed a memorable day.

This avenue of horse chestnut trees, leading to the Melford Bridge, was planted in December 1902 to commemorate the coronation of King Edward VII; the first tree was planted by the Mayor, Mr Charles Burrell, jnr. Known for many years as Coronation Avenue, it is now lined with mature trees and forms part of Castle Street.

CORONATION DAY, 1911

A competition for the best decorated house was held in the town as part of the coronation celebrations in 1902 and again in 1911. Mr Benjamin Duffield, dressed in his Borough of Thetford Fire Brigade uniform, poses outside his home with his wife, Lydia. Now demolished, Ben Duffield's house stood in the area now occupied by the Court House. [Photograph courtesy of Geoff Howlett]

CORONATION DAY, 1911

King Edward VII died in 1910 and his son was crowned King George V in June the following year. Thetford's coronation celebrations began with a parade on the Market Place, followed by a Divine Service in St Peter's Church. In the afternoon a variety of activities were held in the Castle Park, including a ceremony to dedicate the Colours of the 1st Thetford Troop of Boy Scouts. The day finished with a firework display from the top of the Castle Hill. In this photograph Thetford's Boy Scouts, followed by members of local friendly societies, march along a gaily decorated King Street towards St Peter's Church, 22nd June 1911.

CORONATION DAY, 1937

The reign of George V ended with his death at Sandringham in January, 1936. The previous year the nation had celebrated the Silver Jubilee of the King and Queen.

After the turmoil surrounding the abdication of the late King's eldest but uncrowned son, King Edward VIII, Edward's brother was crowned in his place. The coronation of King George VI took place on the 12th May 1937, the date originally planned for the coronation of King Edward VIII.

Thetford's coronation day began with the Mayor, Sir William Gentle, laying a wreath on the War Memorial.

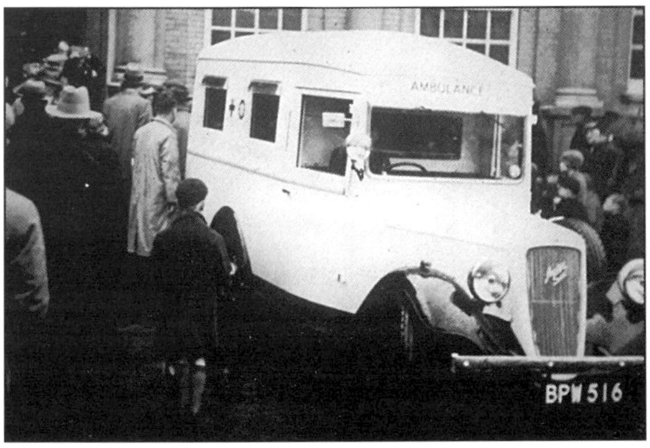

CORONATION DAY, 1937

The dedication and presentation of Thetford's first brand-new, motor ambulance took place on the Market Place as part of the Coronation Day celebrations. The ambulance was purchased for the town by Miss E. Fison and her sister, Mrs K. Mason. A new ambulance station was also built in Earls Street to commemorate the coronation of King George VI.

CORONATION DAY, 1937

Wet weather spoilt the Coronation Day sports held on the 'Rec' [Recreation Ground] in the afternoon. The skies cleared, however, in time for a procession of decorated floats and a fancy dress parade on the Market Place in the early evening. Messrs G. Mower, E. Bowes and H. Clarke entered as *'That Noble Animal'*, the nickname given to the horse used for pulling the corporation refuse-cart. [Photograph courtesy of Alan Clarke]

CORONATION DAY, 1937

Just one of the many decorated floats enters the Market Place from Well Street. Mr Ben Culey, the proprietor of Thetford's Palace Cinema, filmed the local coronation celebrations for posterity. Soon afterwards Thetfordians were able to watch themselves on the 'silver screen'.

ST NICHOLAS STREET, CORONATION DAY, 1953

The coronation of Queen Elizabeth II took place on the 2nd June 1953. Thetford's coronation celebrations began the previous Sunday with an open-air service in the ruined church of the Cluniac Priory. Many other events were organised that week, including a presentation to all the children of Thetford by the Mayor, Mr G. E. Lambert, of a special coronation beaker inscribed with the Borough Coat-of-Arms. Other activities included street parties such as this, organised by residents in the area surrounding St Nicholas Street.

Something new for many Thetfordians on the coronation day was the opportunity to see the coronation 'live' on television. Although Thetford was only on the fringe of the area for receiving television pictures, the St Johns Hall and the club room at the Green Dragon public house were turned into television viewing centres. Three television sets were installed in each place and people began queuing at 7 o'clock in the morning to take advantage of this new attraction. [Photograph courtesy of Eastern Counties Newspapers]

KILVERSTONE ESTATE, 1953

This photograph captures the asparagus pickers' coronation tea party, held in an old barn on the estate. Included in the photograph: Sid Aylott, 'Jock' Brown, Fred Codling, Sylvia Coe, George Hazell, Margaret Hazell, Marjorie Linge, Alice Lockwood, Mrs Maund, Barry Rutterford, Reg Rutterford, 'Midge' Turner, 'Clemmie' Vincent, Mrs Vincent. The asparagus pickers also decorated a lorry with flags and different varieties of asparagus as part of the coronation celebrations [also see page 19].

Since the Thetford Town Development began in the late 1950s part of the Kilverstone Estate now forms a part of Thetford and the village of Kilverstone has become a suburb of the town. [Photograph courtesy of Studio Five, Thetford]

THE QUEEN'S VISIT, 1993

On the 20th May 1993, almost exactly forty years after her coronation, Queen Elizabeth visited Thetford. It is reputed to be the first official visit to the town by a reigning monarch since the first Queen Elizabeth in 1578. Undoubtedly those same timbers of the ancient Bell Hotel, that can be seen in the background, also witnessed the visit of Queen Elizabeth I. [Photograph courtesy of Eastern Counties Newspapers]

KING STREET, 1993

Thousands of cheering and patriotic spectators lined the royal route from the Market Place to St Nicholas Street, where the Queen officially opened 'Breckland House', the new offices of Breckland District Council. Not surprisingly, considering past royal celebrations in the town, the weather was once again unsettled.

The Queen was accompanied by HRH Prince Philip on this visit to Norfolk. The Prince had visited Thetford the previous year when officially opening the Nunnery headquarters of the British Trust for Ornithology. Another royal visitor in the 1980s was the Duchess of Kent who officially opened the Riversdale Centre in 1980 and Rosemary Musker High School in 1984. [Photograph courtesy of Eastern Counties Newspapers]

THE WORKPLACE

'The economy of Thetford was transformed by the town development scheme. The unemployment rate fell steadily, until in 1964 it was only 0.9 per cent., and as late as 1975 it was still below 3 per cent. Thus the industrialisation provided jobs not only for the newcomers but also for the existing unemployed inhabitants of the town'.

Alan Crosby, 'A History of Thetford', published 1986

BIDWELL'S MALTSTERS, 1909

Large quantities of barley, grown in the district of Thetford, were brought into the town for malting; malt is a basic ingredient in the production of beer. Bidwell's, Cronshey's and Fison's all owned extensive maltings early in the 20th century, when most of Thetford's main industrial premises, the maltings, mills, tannery, artificial manure works and the agricultural engineering works of Charles Burrell & Sons Ltd., were centred on the rivers Thet and Little Ouse.

RIVERSIDE MALTINGS, c.1962

Much of the malt processed in Thetford was once transported to London's breweries and elsewhere, by way of barges or 'lighters' on the Little Ouse river. Before the beginning of the 20th century, new malting houses were built, not beside the river, but adjacent to the railway line.

These brick and flint-built maltings were still operating into the 1960s when they were sold by R. & W. Paul Ltd., and demolished to make way for the Riverside Walk development. Very few of Thetford's former maltings remain today. Note the cowls on the roof to allow unwanted heat to escape from the malt kilns.

Still standing, in the right foreground, is the old Tan House purchased by Norfolk County Council in 1950. The tannery closed in the 1920s and in 1960 work began clearing the former tanyard for a car park.

THE PULP WORKS, c.1930

Malting, flour milling and tanning had been carried out in the town for many centuries, while the manufacture of pulp-ware, artificial manure and agricultural machinery were comparatively new industries. This ancient industrial site was originally a flour mill. By the early years of the 18th century it was a paper mill. Pulp-ware, such as hats, bowls and trays, to name but a few items, were first made here in the 1870s. It was the last of the old riverside industrial areas. Manufacture continued here until 1989 when Thetford Moulded Products moved into a new factory on one of the town's northern industrial estates and the old Pulp Mill was demolished. In 1995 work began developing part of the site as a residential estate.

THE PULP WORKS, 1926

In this photograph, bowls and pots are shaped by a hydraulic press. After drying and trimming the pulp-ware was soaked in linseed oil before painting and decorating in a variety of colours and designs. On the left is George Flack and on the right Ethel Brame. In the early years of the century, the Pulp Works was one of the few places in the town that provided regular factory work for women.

THE PITT MILL, 1996

The old, water-powered flour mill, formerly known as Pitt Mill, stands over the river Thet. In 1936, about ten years after flour was last milled there, it was turned into a factory for roasting, grinding and packing coffee. Tea was also processed. This was one of several new industries attracted to Thetford in the 1930s. The Coffee Mill, as it came to be known, closed in 1956 and since the early 1960s has been a Masonic Hall.

from good grocers everywhere

the local product
with a national reputation

The Ibex Coffee Co. Ltd. **The Old Mill, Thetford.**

FISON'S TWO MILE BOTTOM WORKS, c.1910

Fison's works were originally situated in the centre of Thetford, near the Town Bridge but had moved beside the Little Ouse river at Two Mile Bottom, within the borough boundary, in the middle of the 19th century. Fison's TMB Works, as they were known, were an established and important part of the local industrial scene by the beginning of the 20th century. Super phosphates and compound fertilizers were produced there until the acid plant was shut down in 1933. From then until 1950, the works were used for the dry storage of fertilizers and thereafter until closure in 1973, it operated as a bulk storage depot. [Photograph courtesy of the Ancient House Museum, Thetford]

CHARLES BURRELL & SONS LTD, c.1925

Charles Burrell's agricultural engineering and steam engine works was Thetford's largest employer of labour from the mid-19th century into the 20th century but even before the turmoil of the Great War some long established local businesses, including Burrell's, were in decline. In an effort to increase trade immediately after the war, Charles Burrell & Sons became part of a consortium known as Agricultural & General Engineers Ltd. It was not enough, however, to save the company. The post-war economic depression not only marked the closure of the Burrell works in 1929 but also the last remaining brewery, flour mill and tannery.

THE TURNERY, CHARLES BURRELL & SONS, LTD., c.1910

During the economic and industrial problems of the 1920s, Thetford Borough Council sought ways of attracting new industries to the town. Even Henry Ford was approached in an effort to utilise the former Burrell works as a factory for manufacturing motor cars. In an attempt to improve the town's economic fortunes, a Thetford Chamber of Trade and Advancement Association was also formed in 1926. Nonetheless, many former Burrell employees and their families moved away from the town to seek work elsewhere. Between 1921 and 1931 Thetford's population fell from 4,705 to 4,098. This was the first recorded serious decline for many years.

This part of the Burrell works remained empty until occupied by a fruit and vegetable canning company in the late 1940s. [Photograph courtesy of the Charles Burrell Museum, Thetford]

MINSTERGATE, c.1938

In the 1930s part of the St Nicholas Works in Minstergate was given over to the processing of rabbit skins. Another part was utilised as W. & G. Lambert's trailer and coachworks. In this photograph, employees of British Rabbit Industries [formerly H. Bauman] pose outside their Minstergate factory. On the extreme left is Cyril Pearson. Also amongst this group is Charlie Pearson, Cyril's father. [Photograph courtesy of Anne Fuller]

MINSTERGATE, c.1938

Thetford's short-lived rabbit industry, it had ceased by 1940, differed from that at nearby Brandon, a major centre for the rabbit fur trade. At Brandon the rabbit pelts were used for the felt-hat making industry situated elsewhere, while at Thetford the rabbit's belly-fur was preserved and the pelts exported to European coat manufacturers. Local warreners were paid an extra 2d per rabbit, to slit the rabbit between its hind legs rather than the belly. In this view, the skins or pelts have been dried and are now ready for packaging and dispatch. [Photograph courtesy of Anne Fuller]

WARRENERS, c.1905

Warreners could still be found working on local agricultural estates into the 1950s, although rabbits were no longer reared in areas specifically defined as a 'warren'. Gamekeepers and warreners were employed in an attempt to control the large rabbit population, found in local fields, heaths, commons and hedgerows. Not only were rabbits damaging crops, forest plantations and the local landscape, in the early 1950s they upset Thetford's cricketers by burrowing under the pitch on the Recreation Ground.

Local warreners were put out of work after 1953-54, however, when the virus, myxomatosis cuniculus, spread from France to southeast England. Within a few months, Thetford and the Breckland were almost free of the wild rabbit, for a few years at least.

MINSTERGATE, 1963

In 1932, Norfolk Canneries Ltd, began canning fruit and vegetables in buildings that stood just south of the Town Bridge; in 1947-48 they moved to Minstergate, on the opposite side of the river, into the old workshops of Charles Burrell & Sons. Production continued here, providing work for about 150 - sometimes more in the summer time - until 1980 when the canning factory was closed. [Photograph courtesy of Thetford Town Council]

MINSTERGATE, 1985

This photograph shows the former canneries site being cleared for a supermarket and car park. The curved roof of the former Burrell paint shop can be seen. This building was opened as the Charles Burrell Museum in 1991. Beyond is the tower of St Peter's Church.

SIMONS' DAIRY FARM, c.1950

There were several farms scattered about the Borough of Thetford until the early 1960s when hundreds of acres of agricultural land were set aside for the Town Expansion Scheme.

Gerald Simons and his sisters farmed from 57, Bury Road, where the farm house, dairy and milking parlour were situated. The Simons also delivered milk from their Bury Road dairy to local door-steps. Until 1961, it was a common sight to see Simons' herd of cows being driven from a field where Nunsgate now stands, along Mill Lane and on to the Bury Road. In this photograph, Simons' bull stands in the yard; Gerald and one of his sisters can just be seen behind with Wilfred Baldry in the foreground.

T. SIMONS

Thetford Dairy Farm

FOR

All Grades of Milk and Cream

THE ABBEY FARM, 1918

Even if it were often only casual or seasonal employment, farming still provided a considerable amount of work within the Borough and neighbouring parishes, certainly into the middle of the 20th century. The Abbey Farm was one of three farms of about 1,000 acres in the borough. There were also a few smaller ones and numerous small holdings. Early in the century, important local industries such as malting, flour milling and tanning all relied on agriculture for their raw materials, while others supplied the farms with goods and services. Farming ceased on the Abbey Farm in 1962 and early in the following year the farm equipment was auctioned, the farm land ear-marked for development.

This photograph of men at work with their scythes in the harvest fields, was taken near the Water Works on the Mundford Road. Surprisingly, it captures an ancient agricultural scene, for farming was already a highly mechanised industry.

From left-right: T. Smith, Hazlewood, W. Nunn, W. Stearne, B. Gooch, H. Back, G. Ladell, G. Atkins, A. Hazelewood, B. Matthews, J. H. Murton, H. Lockwood, C. Allison, M. Ladell. [Photograph courtesy of Arthur Lockwood]

KILVERSTONE ESTATE, c.1953

Lord Fisher, 2nd Baron of Kilverstone [1920-1955], was the first to start growing asparagus on the 3,000 acre Kilverstone Estate. Besides providing employment for people living in the parish of Kilverstone, many from Thetford found casual work on the estate, picking and packing asparagus, blackcurrants, carrots and other agricultural produce. Most of the asparagus picked at Kilverstone between April - June was taken to Thetford railway station and dispatched to London, some of it to Harrod's store.

A wildlife park was created on part of the Kilverstone Estate by Lord and Lady John Fisher, the 3rd Baron of Kilverstone, in 1973. Kilverstone Wildlife Park specialised in a variety of South American animals until closure in the early 1990s. [Photograph courtesy of Daisy Kenny]

THE CHEQUERS, KING STREET, c.1915

Brewing was an important local industry into the first quarter of the 20th century. This is reflected by the numerous licensed public houses that could be found in the town early in the century. Many of Thetford's 31 public houses were tied to local brewer, Bidwell & Co., of Old Market Street. The Chequers was one of Bidwell's pubs until closure in 1921, three years before the brewery closed. Bidwell's old brewery still survives, while the old Chequers was demolished in 1962 to make way for new shops.

W. BOUGHTON & SONS LTD, BOOKBINDING DEPARTMENT, c.1910

In the first quarter of the century, a wide-range of occupations could also be found away from the industries that lined the river. Between the numerous public houses scattered about the town, there were the small workshops and premises of bakers, blacksmiths, bootmakers, builders, butchers, carriers, carpenters, dressmakers, printers, saddlers and all kinds of shopkeepers, dealers and merchants.

Printing has been a long established local industry, if only of a modest size. W. Boughton & Sons Ltd established an electric printing works on the Station Road in 1897 and continue trading from there today.

HENRY GREEN'S PRINTING WORKS, c.1955

Henry Green's printing works was situated at the rear of his stationery and newsagent's shop [now the Heart Foundation shop] in King Street. From left-right: Percy Green, Percy Ward and Albert George. When Percy Green began as an apprentice here in 1903 his working day was 6 am-5.30 pm with one hour for lunch, from Monday to Friday, and 6 am-1 pm on Saturdays.

Green's was taken over by W. Boughton in 1958 and two years later the printing plant was moved to the Station Road works. The shop continued to trade under the name of Green's until 1984 when it was taken over by a national retailer.

THE GAS WORKS, c.1936

Although the gas works, built on the Bury Road in the 1840s, gave employment to only a small number of men, it provided an invaluable source of energy for lighting and heating the town. This was particularly so in the first half of the century, when Thetford's street lamps were illuminated by gas and many households relied on gas for lighting and cooking. It was 1953 before electric street lamps were introduced into the town, then only along the main roads.

This photograph was taken soon after a new gas-retort house was built. Another major change took place in 1957 when the old coal-gas system was replaced by an oil-gas plant. In the days of the old coal-gas plant, many people will remember queuing at the Gas Works for a barrow-load of coke.

In 1965 a gas pipeline was laid from Norwich to supplement the Thetford plant which was close to running out of capacity. Thetford was also supplying Brandon. Soon afterwards, the Thetford plant was shut down and the town supplied wholly from Norwich. Another major change took place in 1969 when North Sea gas was supplied to the town, just two years after North Sea gas was first fed into Norfolk. It was a well-organised operation. In fourteen days a team of two hundred converted Thetford's nine thousand gas appliances.

The ugly, yet familiar sight of gas holders finally disappeared from the local landscape when the last remaining holder was dismantled in 1989 and six years later the site closed down completely as a gas depot.

THETFORD POST OFFICE, 1939

The present Post Office was opened in May 1939, replacing the adjacent, Late Victorian building that had become inadequate for the needs of the town. It was sometime later, however, before the telephone exchange was installed in the new Post Office. The General Post Office had taken over control of the national telephone system from the National Telephone Company in 1912. In 1939, the Thetford telephone exchange had 296 subscribers.

THE POST OFFICE, c.1950

As can be seen from this photograph of Thetford's postal and telephone staff, the Post Office at Thetford employed a large number of people. Early in the century there were just three town postmen.

The Thetford postal district covered a huge area extending as far north as Shipdham, near Dereham. A manager, thirty-seven postmen, four higher-grade postmen, six part-time postmen, eight counter staff and two cleaners were employed at Thetford Post Office in 1989. Thetford ceased as a mail sorting office in 1994.

Thetford's telephone exchange was also situated at the Post Office until 1970 when a new exchange was opened in Raymond Street. Thetford was then linked to STD (Subscriber Trunk Dialling). Thetford was still without a '999' emergency service until the early 1960s. Other changes include the formation of British Telecommunications in 1981 and the loss of the telegram service in 1982. [Photograph courtesy of Eric Hubbard]

THE COTTAGE HOSPITAL, c.1925 and 1995

Staff working at the Cottage Hospital in Earls Street have been dealing with all sorts of medical conditions for almost a century - the hospital was opened in 1898. Before then, Thetfordians needing major medical treatment had to travel to Bury St Edmunds or Norwich.

Prior to the formation of the National Health Service in 1948, all sorts of local schemes were organised to finance the Cottage Hospital and provide free in-patient care. Since the wards closed to patients in 1964 the hospital has been enlarged to provide numerous out-patient and day-care services.

ST BARNABAS HOSPITAL STAFF, c.1960

St Barnabas Hospital was situated in the former Thetford Union Workhouse. It provided refuge and care for the aged homeless and very poor until 1953. From then until closure in 1970 it was a hospital for the aged infirm. There were then beds for about 60 patients, male and female, and most of the old workhouse wards were either empty or used as storerooms. The small workhouse chapel erected in the 1860s was dedicated to St Barnabas.

Back row, left-right: Mrs Oliver [cook], Edna Greenough, Gladys Ashby, Judy Purt, Violet Mortimer, Maggie Page, Winnie Parslow, Maud Eddington, Ida Musset, Elsie Daisley, Peggy Taylor.

Front row, left-right: Horace Stagg, Molly Anstice, Mrs Broadfoot [sister], Mr Hurd [master], Mrs Hurd [matron], Alma Sheldrake, Eva Bates, Leslie Spiddy. [Photograph courtesy of Garry Burrell]

FARADAY PLACE, c.1962

This block of eight factory units was built in 1959 the first under the Town Development Act. They were ideal premises for small, specialist businesses relocating from London and elsewhere. Between 1959-69 over fifty different sized businesses, manufacturing and processing a wide-range of goods and products, had established themselves on Thetford's new industrial estates, built on the outskirts of the town. Some firms soon expanded into larger factories, but for a variety of reasons, not all were successful. Within a few months or years of arriving in Thetford, several businesses had ceased trading. Nonetheless, employment opportunities for the local workforce had increased enormously. Gradually through the 1960s, 70s and 80s Thetford's old industrial sites along the river side and in the back streets of the town centre disappeared. [Photograph courtesy of Thetford Town Council]

FARADAY PLACE, c.1962

Dress and gown makers, R. E. Moore & Co., began production at Faraday Place in 1960, employing many local girls. In the early 1960s with no big factories in the town employing large numbers of women, except the canneries and pulp works, there were few problems recruiting female labour. However, once firms such as Baxter's Laboratories and Danepak began production in the mid-1960s, it was soon apparent that there was a severe shortage of local female labour. This problem continued into the 1970s despite a number of schemes designed to improve the situation. More recent economic, social and technological changes, however, have to an extent resolved some earlier labour problems. [Photograph courtesy of Thetford Town Council]

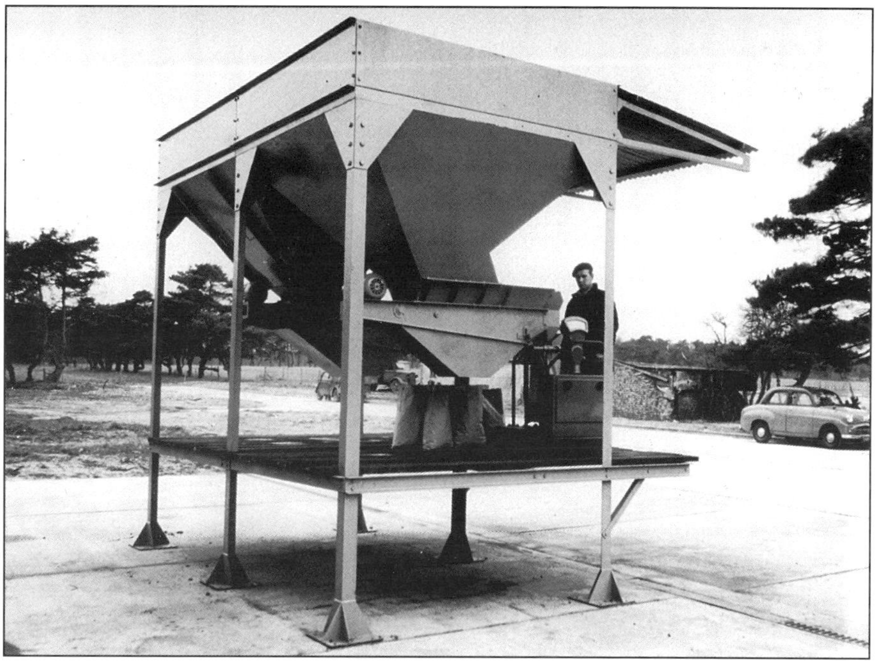

J. A. CLARK & CO. [ENGINEERS] LTD., c.1959

Two of the first firms to move on to the new industrial estates were cold store and freezer equipment manufacturer, G. Williams Engineering Co. Ltd, and J. A. Clark, who produced coal hoppers and other general fabrication work. In 1961 a link was made with an earlier part of Thetford's industrial scene when the Trustees of Sir Joseph Williamson's Charity, founded in 1718 for *'binding poor children belonging to the Borough of Thetford'*, apprenticed two local boys to J. A. Clark & Co.

In this view the remains of farm buildings can still be seen behind one of Clarke's coal hoppers. The trackway is now Stephenson Way and the surrounding fields are occupied by industrial premises. [Photograph courtesy of J. A. Clark & Co.]

NOVABORD [UK] LTD, BURRELL WAY, 1963

In 1961, it was announced that a large timber processing plant was to be built on the London Road industrial estate. Two years later the new £2 million pound factory, with an annual production capacity of about 17 million square feet of particle wood board, was opened by Sir Geoffrey Ripon, M.P. Sadly, despite early optimism, from the start it was a venture plagued with all sorts of problems. Within two years of opening, it had been taken over by Airscrew Weyroc and in 1965 the plant was closed down for nearly two years after an explosion killed a worker. Production finally ceased in 1980.

Between 1981-91, the site was privately developed into a business park, occupied by a variety of retail and industrial companies. An efficient waste disposal and recycling plant was also opened on the site in the early 1980s, replacing rubbish skips that had been sited on land in front of the old St Barnabas Hospital. [Photograph courtesy of Thetford Town Council]

LONDON ROAD INDUSTRIAL ESTATE, 1995

It is over thirty-five years since the first factories were built on this estate, so beginning the Town Development scheme and a new era in Thetford's industrial fortunes. The first factories to be built were those in the bottom half of the picture, backing on to Beech Close and Rowan Close. From there the factories gradually spread south and westwards, although, on the opposite side of the London Road, construction work also began at an early date with Thermos in the upper-centre of the photograph opening early in 1965. Later that same year Baxter's Laboratories and Danepak, both employing large workforces, opened close by.

Most of the factory premises in this view have expanded since first opening, while others have changed ownership and use. Thetford's industries now manufacture an extensive range of products, employing Thetfordians and many people from a wide area of Norfolk and Suffolk.

In the top-left of this view can be seen the Forest Retail Park and in the opposite corner the Brandon Road and Thetford Golf Club. [Photograph by Derek A. Edwards (courtesy of Norfolk Museum Services), 19 June 1995. Ref: TL8582/KHBV8]

BURRELL WAY, 1991

Fire has damaged or destroyed a number of Thetford's industrial premises during the 20th century. Some of the most notable blazes include: Burrell's St Nicholas Works - 1922, Pulp Mill -1928, Goddard's building yard in Station Road - 1946, Thermos factory - 1965, Conran's warehouse [former maltings] Station Road -1968, Nichol Beauty Products - 1970, former maltings Raymond Street - 1980, former maltings Croxton Road - 1980 and Fogarty's Minstergate factory - 1986.

This fire at D. & L. Plastics in October 1991 was described by senior fire officers as *'one of the worst blazes they had ever had to tackle in Norfolk'*. Over 200 fire-fighters from all over East Anglia were in attendance over a period of three days before the fire was finally extinguished. Fortunately, the pall of toxic smoke from the burning plastic, drifted away from the centre of the town. It was 1995 before the site was declared free from toxic contamination. [Photograph courtesy of Eastern Counties Newspapers Ltd.]

FISON WAY INDUSTRIAL ESTATE, 1982

Thetford's industries have produced a great variety of valuable and useful articles but none can have been quite as fabulous as the probable 4th-5th century hoard of Roman gold and silver artefacts and jewellery, discovered while the foundations for this Travenol warehouse were being prepared in November 1979. The 'Thetford Treasure' is now on display in the British Museum, London, while Thetford's Ancient House Museum displays part of a replica treasure.

Aerial photographs of the Gallows Hill area taken a few months after the discovery of the Thetford Treasure revealed interesting rectangular crop-marks, just to the north of the warehouse site. When this photograph was taken, archaeologists were excavating the site. They discovered an intriguing system of rectangular enclosures, built in several stages, surrounding three round buildings and two similar structures. The site has been interpreted as some kind of Iceni tribal or religious centre. It appears to have been destroyed before completion about the time of the Iceni's uprising against the Romans, AD 60-70. [Photograph by Derek A. Edwards (courtesy of Norfolk Museum Services), 30 March 1982. Ref: TL8685/ABE/ARU3]

FISON WAY INDUSTRIAL ESTATE, 1988

Fison Way was the fourth industrial estate to be built when work began in the early 1970s. In the bottom-right foreground is the Travenol warehouse seen on the previous page. It is now used by Jeyes. A part of Jeyes' factory, where production began in 1970 making toilet rolls and a range of household cleaning products, can be seen top-right of the view. In the centre-foreground is TNT's Lodge Way depot. Howlett Way can be seen running diagonally across the view, past the rows of Deutz Fahr tractors and combine harvesters waiting to be distributed. Like several other industrial premises in this view, the Deutz Fahr site is now [1995] waiting to be let or sold, a victim of recent industrial recession. Howlett Way is linked to the Mundford Road by Fison Way. This industrial scene was unimaginable to most Thetfordians just four decades ago. Likewise, it is as equally difficult to predict with certainty, Thetford's long-term industrial future. [Photograph by Derek A. Edwards (courtesy of Norfolk Museum Services), 8 July 1988.
Ref: L8684/GDVC6]

ON THE ROAD

'The question of street watering on Sundays was again discussed. It was stated that it was most needed on the old turnpike roads, London, White Hart Street and Norwich Road. On a recent Sunday there were 15 "obnoxious motor cars" passing this route during divine service, which proved "an interminable nuisance both as to noise and dust," and if the route could be watered from 8 to 10am., on the Sunday it would add to the comfort of those who attend the various places of worship'.

From a report of the Special Meeting of Thetford Town Council and Urban District Council, July, 1906. Published in the Bury Free Press, 21 July 1906

WHITE HART STREET, c.1910

In the early years of the 20th century White Hart Street formed the main thoroughfare. All sorts of horse-drawn vehicles, adapted to carry anything from small parcels to barrels of beer or huge tree trunks, could be seen on the roads of Thetford. The horseless carriage or motor car, as it came to be known, was still a rarity.

THE POST OFFICE, c.1915

It is estimated by one contemporary early in the 20th century, that local businesses and individuals owned at least 160 horses between them. Blacksmiths, coachmakers and painters, farriers, harness and saddlemakers, wheelwrights and others were all busily employed keeping the horse and cart on the road. In this view a horse-drawn mail van, contracted by the Post Office from a local carrier, stands outside the Post Office built in 1894. Local carriers also ran regular journeys to surrounding towns and villages, usually departing from Thetford's inns and public houses.

JAMES FISON & SONS LTD., 1912

Fison's head horseman, Charlie Baker, is about to set off for the Royal Norfolk Show with a wagon loaded with Fison's special barley manure. The Norfolk Show was held at Thetford in 1912 and again in 1924. The decorated building in the background is Benjamin Duffield's house [also illustrated on page 8]. The sign reads 'SUCCESS TO AGRICULTURE'.

Fison's used horses at Thetford until the early 1930s when motor lorries were introduced. [Photograph courtesy of Geoff Howlett]

THE WHITE HORSE INN, c.1915

By the time that this photograph was taken, motor vehicles were already becoming a common sight about the town. As the number of horses dwindled becoming difficult to obtain for hire, the local fire brigade often encountered the serious problem of finding horses to pull the steam fire engine when called to fight a fire. The Fire Brigade overcame this problem to some extent in the 1920s when an arrangement was made to tow the steam fire engine with a local coal merchant's motor lorry, even if loaded with coal.

The White Horse Inn, situated in Raymond Street, was appropriately one of the last local inns from where horses and carriages could be hired. [Photograph courtesy of Mary Clarke]

CASTLE PARK, c.1910

When this photograph was taken by Roger Bantock, cycling was a very popular mode of transport and pastime for both sexes of all ages, even though new cycles were relatively expensive. The clothes and headdress these young ladies are wearing would be considered entirely unsuitable for cycling today.

The earliest known reference to cycling in the vicinity of Thetford is 1878, when a cyclist was reported to have caused an accident by frightening a horse pulling a cart on the road between Barnham and Thetford. There have been a number of cycling clubs in the town since then, the first being formed in the 1890s.

ST NICHOLAS STREET, c.1959

Like the hand-cart, bicycles were adapted to carry all sorts of goods. In this photograph, Jimmy Hume is about to set-off from his St Nicholas Street home, delivering Sunday newspapers about the town and neighbouring villages. [Photograph courtesy of Gladys Blackburn]

PETER FRANCIS, 1968

Perhaps Thetford's best known and remembered newspaper 'boy' is Peter Francis, who cycled thousands of miles around Thetford and the surrounding villages after he began his paper rounds in 1949. [Photograph courtesy of Eastern counties Newspapers]

THE CO-OP BAKERY, ST NICHOLAS STREET, c.1905

Besides horse-drawn vehicles and the bicycle, a popular and economical way of conveying goods about the town was the humble hand-cart and wheelbarrow. Carts were used by all sorts of roundsmen and traders such as bakers, builders, butchers, general dealers, and milkmen. The hand-cart also had another practical purpose in the early years of the century, before Thetford could afford a proper motor ambulance. People needing urgent medical treatment were often conveyed to the Cottage Hospital on the nearest available cart.

HENRY KNIGHTS, c.1930

Henry 'Henny' Knights, rag and bone merchant of Pike Lane, was a familiar figure pushing his barrow about the streets of the town in the 1920s and 30s. While some hand-carts may have been specially made by a coach builder, Henny's was almost certainly constructed from salvaged materials.

MAGDALEN STREET, 1935

Mr Robert Pert's milkman, Harry Johnson, delivered milk about the town from this hand-cart, decorated for Thetford's Silver Jubilee celebrations in May 1935. The frequent sight of hand-carts and wheelbarrows about the town did not really disappear until well into the 1950s. By then the horse, pulling carts and wagons on local roads and even working on the farms, was no more than a memory.

KING STREET, 1995

The hand-cart can still be seen on odd occasions about the town in late 20th century Thetford. This distinguished looking gentleman, Mr David 'Pat' Plummer of Hepworth, can occasionally be seen in King Street using the chassis of a pram as a hand-cart, to carry and help spread the words of Jesus Christ.

AA PATROLMAN, c.1925

Soon after its introduction, the internal combustion engine was being adapted to power bicycles. As a result, the motor cycle was born. And as much for economical reasons, the motor cycle proved to be a popular mode of transport, even if it was a more precarious ride than the motor car.

The AA [Automobile Association], founded in 1905, soon adopted motor cycles for their road patrol service. Herbert Osborne of Thetford is seen on duty at nearby Elveden with his Norton motor cycle and side-car.

THE MILL STREAM CAFE, c.1967

The 1960s saw an increasing number of young men in particular, riding high-powered motor cycles and forming informal fraternities. Thetford's Millstream Café [now the Retreat public house] was such a meeting place for motor cyclists and young people in the 1960s and early 70s.

These young men are in the road opposite the café, a scene that has changed drastically in recent years. In the distant background is the St John's Hall. [Photograph courtesy of Marcus Bunning]

THE "BURRELL" STEAM WAGON, 1911

With the town being a centre for the manufacture of Charles Burrell's steam-powered engines, Thetfordians and their horses had become well accustomed to the sight and sound of traction engines rumbling through the narrow streets of the town well before the early 1900s. Less than half-a-century earlier, however, one fervent critic described the traction engine, *'a hideous monster belching forth steam and flames and uttering noises that would terrify the most perfectly broken animal'*. Perhaps that same gentleman would be pleased to know that none of the 113 steam wagons or lorries made by Burrell's between 1911-1928 have survived.

DORAN BROS., LTD, c.1920

Former Burrell employee, Thomas R. Doran [1868-1940] began as a steam rolling and steam haulage contractor from his Croxton Road premises in 1896. From one horse and one engine, his business expanded to a fleet of about fifteen steam rollers by the 1930s. After the war many of these engines became redundant and stood for several years in Doran's yard. Most were eventually sold for scrap but a few were preserved, including this 10 ton roller built in 1911.

DORAN'S STEAM ROLLERS, GUILDHALL STREET, c.1910

From photographs taken early in the twentieth century, it is clear that Thetford's roads were very rough, even the main roads were untarred. Tramps passing through the local workhouse were often given the task of breaking heaps of granite into small pieces for use on the roads. It was not until after many years' work by the local authorities, who contracted firms such as Thomas Doran, that road surfaces gradually improved.

Although the sight and sound of steam-powered road locomotives and lorries had become less common after the 1930s, steam rollers could still be seen working in Thetford well into the 1950s.

MR BOUGHTON'S MOTOR CAR, c.1900

Motor vehicles began to make their appearance in Thetford about the turn of the century. This French-built De Dion-Bouton, owned by Mr Walter Boughton, snr, is believed to be the first motor car in Thetford. Another member of the Boughton family, Walter, jnr, has the probable distinction of being the first person in Thetford to be prosecuted for a motoring offence. He was fined in July 1900 after travelling at 12-13 mph in Guildhall Street.

W. & G. LAMBERT, MOTOR ENGINEERS, c.1926

In the early years of the century, not everyone welcomed the motor car, especially on days when the roads were dry and dusty. Nonetheless the internal-combustion engine was here to stay. As the stable doors slowly closed, local businesses and individuals gradually purchased a motor vehicle of some kind. This Ford 'Model T' was owned by Lambert's of Castle Street and hired to the Post Office for the collection and delivery of the Royal Mail within the Thetford postal district. It was 1936 before the local post office operated its own fleet of motor vans.

There was little comfort for drivers and passengers of vehicles such as this, particularly on cold, dark wintry nights. The tyres were made of solid rubber and there were no windscreen wipers or cab heaters. The vehicle lighting was provided by acetylene lamps that were prone to be extinguished in wet and windy weather. When the petrol tank was nearly empty, the driver often had to negotiate steep hills in reverse, so that the force of gravity allowed petrol to reach the carburetter.

THE MARKET PLACE, c.1923

Some time in the early 1920s, a Thetford & District Motor and Motor Cycle Club was formed. This photograph is believed to have been taken before they set off on a road-run to Framlingham in April 1923. Most members of the Thetford Motor Club and owners of these vehicles were local businessmen and the wealthier section of the town and district.

Car ownership continued to increase through the 1930s even though driving tests for motorists were introduced in 1934 and a 30 m.p.h. limit imposed in built-up areas. It was the 1950s before the dream of a family car became a reality for many more people. Even so, probably no more than one in twenty families in the town owned a motor car in 1960. [Photograph courtesy of Brian Boughton]

MILL LANE, c.1935

Before 1930, when Lord Iveagh of Elveden Hall loaned the town this 1910 Mercedes motor for pulling the steam fire engine, the Borough Fire Brigade relied on horses or a local coalman's lorry to haul the fire engine when called to a fire. This system continued until 1938 when a brand-new Dennis motor fire engine was purchased for the town and district. That same year the Corporation purchased a motorised dust or refuse cart to replace the horse-drawn vehicle. Needless to say, the Corporation night-soil 'honey' wagon continued to be horse-drawn until after the war. [Photograph courtesy of East Anglian Film Archive]

RAYMOND STREET, c.1935

The horse and cart could still be seen in the mid-1930s when this photograph was taken of the Thetford Co-operative Society's transport fleet. These vehicles were used to deliver a wide-range of goods to customers, including door-to-door deliveries of bread, coal and groceries. The Co-op first purchased a motor van in 1922 for deliveries around the surrounding countryside. That same year the Co-op's stables in Raymond Street were demolished and replaced with a garage.

PAULS' MALTINGS, BRIDGE STREET, 1949

As the century progressed, motor-powered road haulage vehicles increased in size and power. This 1947 five ton Austin lorry was considered a fairly large motor vehicle in its day. Before the introduction of bulk haulage it was used for transporting sacks of malt from Thetford to Ipswich and other East Anglian towns. [Photograph courtesy of Geoff Howlett]

EDMONDS' MOTORS, c.1925

In the early years of the twentieth century the horse-drawn carriage for passenger travel was succeeded by the motor car and the open-topped, motor char-à-banc, and then the covered saloon motor coach. This photograph provides evidence of that transition from char-à-banc to motor coach. The body work was made in the mid-1920s by Edmonds' Motors of Croxton Road, Thetford. They had gone out of business by 1931.

DORAN'S LUXURY SALOON COACHES, c.1935

Thetford's first motor coach proprietors were Allison's of White Hart Street and Doran's of Croxton Road. Derek Doran, one of Thomas Doran's two sons, began operating a bus service in 1929 and in 1947 he formed his own limited company: Coach Services [1947] Thetford Limited. In 1969, Mr Doran sold the business which still operates from Croxton Road today.

EASTERN COUNTIES BUS, c.1960

An Eastern Counties bus, on the 255 Thetford - Bury St Edmunds service, stands outside Thetford railway station. The Eastern Counties Omnibus Co. Ltd first began operating a regular round-the-town bus service in April 1964. [Photograph courtesy of D. Withers, Bristol Vintage Bus Group]

THETFORD COACH STATION, 1995

Until the bus and coach station was established here, at the Riverside, in 1974, Thetford's Market Place acted as an impromptu station for local and long distance coaches. In this photograph an Eastern Counties mini bus is about to depart for the London Road Estates; the 'Mini line' service commenced in 1988. A double-decker bus for Newmarket stands alongside.

LAMBERTS' GARAGE, CASTLE STREET, c.1935

Certainly by the 1920s several garages, providing the many services demanded by the increasing number of motorists, had become established along the main roads through the town. The main garage in Thetford was W. & G. Lambert Ltd of Castle Street. W. Lambert began as a coach builder in the days before the motor car. Lamberts' business gradually expanded with branch garages on the Norwich Road and Guildhall Street and workshops in Minstergate. Lamberts' business was taken over by Duff Morgan & Vermont Ltd in 1968.

In 1996, part of Lambert's former premises, including the ornate gabled showroom on the right of this view, were demolished as part of a new Peddars Way residential development on land at the rear and once Nickerson's woodyard.

RAY POWELL'S GARAGE, BURY ROAD, 1994

Lamberts' closest rival, Hanbury & Co., was situated in these premises on what was the London Road. In the previous century they were occupied by coach builder, Alfred Palmer. From 1948 until 1972 Hanbury's old garage was occupied by T. H. Nice of Bury St Edmunds. Since the late 1970s, after being vacant for a few years, the premises have been occupied and modernised firstly by the Thetford Motor Company and from the mid-1980s by the Ray Powell Group, recently acquired by Whichford. The original part of the garage can be seen on the right. The road passing in front of Nice's old garage, now part of Newtown, was the main A11 road until 1968 when the 'inner-relief' road was opened.

KING STREET, 1955

Thetford's traffic problems continued to worsen with the steady increase of motor traffic during the 1950s. To alleviate some of the town centre problems, King Street the main commercial street, Tanner Street and Well Street were created 'One Way' in 1957. King Street remained open to 'One Way' traffic until early in 1974 when workmen began pedestrianising the street from east of the Kings House to the Market Place. [Photograph courtesy of Thetford Town Council]

BRIDGE STREET, 1959

A typical scene on a Saturday during the summer holiday period in the 1950s and 60s, the 'Bell Corner' and Bridge Street congested with motor traffic. Even though traffic lights were installed at the notorious 'Bell Corner' in the mid-1930s, the narrow Bridge Street and White Hart Street continued to be the cause of numerous traffic 'jams' on the main A11 road through the town. In 1960 it was reported that over 1,500 vehicles an hour were passing through the town on the A11 towards Newmarket on Saturdays during the summer holiday season. [Photograph courtesy of Eastern Counties Newspapers]

BURY ROAD, 1962

Private car ownership was, at least in Thetford, an exception to the rule for most families well into the 1960s. This 1958 Ford Consul was the Atkins' family car, and was used mainly for pleasure outings and drives at weekends. Like many owners of a family car at that time, Bert Atkins and his family continued to rely on bicycles or 'shank's pony' for every-day travel about the town. A marked difference from today, when most families depend on the car for almost every journey. [Photograph courtesy of Denise Jones]

NORWICH ROAD, 1967

Many of the buildings that can be seen in Station Road, Painter Street and the north end of White Hart Street are about to be demolished as work begins on the 'inner-relief road'. Although the new 'inner-relief road' solved some of the traffic problems experienced before opening in October 1968, it was soon apparent from the demands of Thetford's increasing population and number of motorists, that a bypass taking traffic well away from the town would have to be built.

NORWICH ROAD, 1994

A view of the busy 'inner-relief road' over a quarter of a century after opening. Despite the opening of the bypass in 1989 complaints continue that heavy goods vehicles still use the route of the old A11 through the town.

It is interesting to note that Thetford's only controlled pedestrian crossing can be seen. It replaced an earlier Zebra crossing, positioned where the photographer was standing. Thetford was one of the first places in the country to display continental-type road signs when introduced early in 1965.

THETFORD BYPASS, 1989

Calls for a Thetford bypass began to be made as far back as the mid-1930s. It was over fifty years later, however, before a bypass became a reality. After much debate, a northern route was decided and construction work began on the 18th April 1988. Despite loud and long calls for a bypass, only a small number of Thetfordians and a Burrell traction engine were there for the opening ceremony on the 13th November 1989. In this view looking north, construction work is in progress at the Brandon Road junction, May 1989.

BURY ROAD, 1993

Despite improvements to the local road system, many Thetfordians continue to suffer from excessive noise and pollution from large volumes of motor traffic, particularly heavy goods vehicles, passing close to their homes. In this photograph taken in October 1993, residents from the Bury Road and neighbouring areas, have brought traffic to a halt as they protest against the number of lorries that use the Bury Road each day. Not only was traffic brought to a stand-still on the Bury Road for 45 minutes, the resulting chaos quickly spread to other local roads. [Photograph courtesy of Bury Free Press]

RAILWAY EXCURSIONS

'If a member of a family ever had travelled as far as London and lived there a short time, we who were juveniles would sit and listen with our eyes and ears open and our mouths agape at the wonderful rehearsal of London life. By an excellent train service we can now step into a covered carriage that is lightsome, airy, clean and comfortable, and ride to London in one third of the time and at one third of the cost, as by the old coach.'

A letter from Robert Nurse of Thetford to the Editor of the Thetford & Watton Times, 1888

THETFORD STATION, c.1910

When the twentieth century began, the Great Eastern Railway had already been running for over half a century through Thetford, on the route between Norwich and Ely. Thetford continued to be a busy station and goods depot into the 1960s, even though the railway was nationalised in 1948 and part of the local rail net-work axed in the early 1950s. Both platforms at the main Thetford railway station were often crowded with people waiting for trains, luggage, mail bags, and all sorts of small, carriagable goods such as crates of live chickens, ducks and boxes of agricultural produce.

W. H. SMITH'S BOOKSTALL, THETFORD STATION, c.1908

Smith's bookstall was once a familiar and welcomed distraction on the platform. It had changed very little from the time this photograph was taken, to the time it was closed and dismantled in 1971. On busy days, passengers would crowd around the bookstall, buying newspapers, books, magazines, cigarettes and sweets to take with them on their journey. Smith's also delivered daily newspapers about the town and it is from here that Peter Francis worked for many years as a newspaper 'boy' [also see page 31].

THETFORD STATION FROM CROXTON ROAD, c.1912 & 1995

The goods sidings and yards at each end of the station were once a scene of great activity as the contents of coal and other wagons were unloaded on to road vehicles for delivery in Thetford and the surrounding district. Moreover, all sorts of goods were dispatched by rail from Thetford and there were frequent goods trains passing through the station both during the day and night time. Some of these trains were mixed goods but others carried nothing but coal, cattle, petrol, frozen fish and other products. By the late 1970s, the railway sidings east and west of the station had become completely obsolete.

In 1995 the cylinderical shape of a 'Sprint' inter-city train approaches the station from the direction of Norwich and past the land east of the station that was eventually sold for redevelopment. In 1992 a new housing estate appropriately known as 'The Sidings' was built on the site. Another new residential development known as Ben Culey Drive was also built immediately to the south, on land once occupied by malt houses.

RAILWAY STATION STAFF, c.1900

The railway staff in this photograph number twenty-two men and two horses. The horses were used for shunting wagons about the goods sidings and are believed to have been used until about 1945. The gentleman in the centre of the middle row is Mr A. C. Sainty, the Station Master. Either side sits Mr Day, the head clerk, and Mr Denny. Where they are sitting was originally the position of a level crossing, carrying the main road to Mundford across the line. It was removed and the road closed after a new road was built in the 1880s, linking the Croxton Road to the Mundford Road north of the station.

RAILWAY STAFF, 1922

When this photograph was taken there were at least fifty men employed by the Great Eastern Railway at Thetford and Thetford Bridge Station. These included station and goods staff, signalmen and maintenance staff. In 1960 there were still about this number but the last thirty years has seen a drastic decline.

Sitting in the front row, from left-right: Mr Denny, Bob Armes, T. Wilby, J. Paul, Mr Bunn [station master], W. Land, F. Goddard, V. Thompson. Also in the photograph is Walter Hiller and George Clarke, the two drivers of the railway company's horse-drawn delivery wagons.

THETFORD STATION, c.1955

'Thetford, Thetford, Thetford. Calling at Harling Road, Eccles Road, Attleborough, Spooner Row, Wymondham, Hethersett and Norwich. Change at Norwich for Lowestoft and Yarmouth'. Once a familiar call from the duty porter as stopping trains for Norwich approached the platform.

Class C12 4-4-2T No. 67360 piloted by Class D 16/3 4-4-0 No. 62564 pulls out of Thetford station with a stopping passenger train for Norwich. Viewed from the Croxton Road bridge, it is a scene that evokes memories of a past railway era. When this photograph was taken, all trains passing through the town were hauled by steam locomotives. [Photograph courtesy of the late George Wells]

THETFORD WEST JUNCTION, c.1955

Class K3 2-6-0 No. 61971 and BR 'Britannia' Pacific 4-6-2 No. 70030 *William Wordsworth* double-head a Norwich-London express past Thetford West Junction signal box. Out of view, just east of the signal box, is the branch line to Thetford Bridge station and Bury St Edmunds. This photograph was taken from Vicarage Road, just east of the Croxton Road bridge and is a scene barely recognisable today, after a concrete road bridge was built across the railway at this point in 1972.

The diesel locomotives and rail-cars introduced in the mid-1950s were doing the bulk of the work within five years. Steam locomotives were a rare sight passing through Thetford by 1961 and in the following year steam-power on the Eastern Region was finally phased-out. [Photograph courtesy of the late George Wells]

THETFORD STATION, 1962

A diesel rail-car stands at the platform. It is the late afternoon service calling at Wretham & Hockham, Stow Bedon, Watton, Holme Hale and Swaffham. Most of the passengers on this particular train were pupils from Thetford Grammar School returning home.

British Railways first experimented with diesels on the Thetford - Swaffham branch line, the 'Crab & Winkle' as it was known, in 1955. Soon after they had replaced steam engines altogether. The service between Thetford and Swaffham closed in June 1964.

THETFORD STATION, 1963

Diesel locomotives were first seen hauling goods and passenger trains through Thetford in 1957. This class of locomotive: English Electric Type 4 weighing 130 tons, was first built in 1958. They were introduced on the Eastern Region to replace the 'Britannia' Class of steam locomotive, hauling express trains between Norwich and London. This train is on the Lowestoft - York service.

THETFORD STATION, 1979

A special excursion, hauled by a diesel locomotive, speeds through Thetford carrying holiday makers to the East Coast. On Saturdays, between the middle of June and early September in the 1950s-70s, special non-stop express trains would pass through Thetford every few minutes, carrying holiday makers to and from the Midlands and the North of England and Great Yarmouth or Lowestoft. Holidays became possible for many more people after the 1939-45 War when firms began providing holidays with pay for all employees.

Apart from the change in motive power, it would appear from this view that there have been few changes from that of seventy years earlier. [Photograph courtesy of John C. Baker]

THE BRIDGE STATION, c.1910

Thetford's second railway station was built east of the town, near the ancient Melford Bridge, for the opening of the railway between Thetford and Bury St Edmunds in 1876. The Thetford - Bury St Edmunds line was part of a link between Colchester and Kings Lynn. The section between Thetford and Bury experienced one of its busiest periods during the 1939-45 War when several thousand tons of bombs and explosives were transported into nearby RAF Barnham.

Before the line was closed to passenger service in 1953, many local children experienced their first rail journey travelling, as a special treat, between the Bridge Station and Thetford's main line station. The line to Bury St Edmunds finally closed to goods services in 1960 and the trackway removed. In the mid-1970s much of the route of the old railway line between the Bridge Station and the main line was made into a roadway, linking the Diss Road with the Norwich Road. In 1992 this road was named Hurth Way, commemorating Thetford's twin-town in Germany.

THE BRIDGE STATION & YOUTH HOSTEL, c.1959

The Bridge Station was utilised as a Youth Hostel in 1955, the only YH in the country to be found in a railway station. It continued to provide accommodation for people exploring Thetford and the surrounding Breckland until closure in 1971.

This photograph was published as a picture postcard about a year before the line was finally closed. The message on the back was written by someone touring the area on a cycle in June 1959 and describes something of the hostel... *'The hostel [hired between 5pm to 10am to the YHA] holds 16 people - 28 of us slept here on Sat. night!'*.

The old Bridge Station still stands beside a busy traffic round-about, its future undecided.

CHILDREN

'Manners and customs have changed much in 60 years. This generation approaches its elders with less awe; as their predecessors shed gloves, they have shed stockings and, in summer, hats, and the gymnastic class which followed Sergeant Ashurst with his flute in 1895 would scarcely have believed their eyes could they have glimpsed into the future and seen a 1948 class in sun tops and knickers'.

Miss E. Gibbs, Headmistress of the Girls' Grammar School, in a foreword to the school magazine, 'The Thetfordian', published 1948

THE MARKET PLACE, c.1905

To-day's childhood is so different from that at the beginning of the 20th century and even that of thirty years ago. Children's games, toys, heroes and heroines change from one generation to another. Each age has new aspirations and dreams and very soon the childhood of one generation becomes the 'old fashioned days' and history for another.

When these children posed for the photographer, most of them could probably boast that they were Thetford born and most probably in the family home. Very few babies come into the world in Thetford today, most are born in a maternity ward of the nearby West Suffolk Hospital, Bury St Edmunds.

1st THETFORD [CONGREGATIONAL] Co., BOYS' BRIGADE, c.1945

Certainly since the early years of the 20th century many different organisations have been formed to nurture and satisfy the needs of children and young people. Perhaps it is not surprising, considering their role, that many of the first youth clubs and organisations were connected to local churches and schools. One of the first national groups in the town was the Young Men's Christian Association. In 1905 they opened premises in White Hart Street, before moving to new, purpose-built quarters in Magdalen Street. Thetford's YMCA closed in 1968 and is now the Conservative Club. Another group closely attached to local churches was this company of the Boys' Brigade who met at the Congregational Chapel, Earls Street where this photograph was taken. Back row: R. Young, C. Grey, H. Langley, G. Osborne, H. Scott, C. Sage, J. Goddard, A. Bibby, D. Babington, R. Boughen. Centre: J. Kendle, D. Kerry, W. Woodhead, W. Reeve, L. Green, Rev. C. Baker, J. Lockwood, N. Vincent, R. Rickwood. Front: A. Flint, A. Kerry, G. Fagg, D. Arnold, A. Bidwell, P. Bidwell, C. Germany, J. Sage, W. James. [Photograph courtesy of Cecil Germany]

THETFORD BOY SCOUT TROOP, 1912

Youth groups were also established through the efforts of individuals like Mr James Edgell of the King's House, and Mr Rowland Palmer, a teacher at the Norwich Road School. They each formed a boy scout troop in the town between 1910-11. The Boy Scout movement founded by Robert Baden-Powell in 1908 has done much to teach boys good citizenship, new skills and the experience of adventure. This photograph was probably taken in the garden of the King's House.

THETFORD GIRL GUIDES, c.1925

The Guide movement began in 1910 with aims similar to those of the Boy Scouts. Seven years later the 1st Thetford Guide Company was formed by Miss Augusta Bidwell and Miss May Green. It appears, however, that this was not the first company of guides to have been formed in the town. A company is known to have been formed at the Girls' Grammar School a few months earlier.

In the 1930s, Thetford's young people were also encouraged to join organisations such as the British Red Cross Society and the St John Ambulance Brigade. Both groups then played an important role in the welfare of the town.

THETFORD GIRL GUIDES, 1984

Each year Thetford's Girl Guides, Boy Scouts and other young people take part in the Remembrance Day parade. In this photograph the guides parade along King Street, having taken part at the special service and wreath-laying ceremony on the Market Place. Taking the salute on a dais against St Cuthbert's Church is the Mayor, supported by Thetford Town Council. In 1995 the Chairman of Breckland District Council, Mr Colin Armes, cut a turf to officially mark the beginning of the construction of the Bidwell Guide & Scout Activity Centre at Two Mile Bottom. When completed, it will provide excellent accommodation and training facilities for guides and scouts.

THETFORD ST. JOHN AMBULANCE BRIGADE, 1975

A unit of the St. John Ambulance Brigade, consisting of adults and young people, was first formed at Thetford in 1937 by the Mayor, Sir William Gentle, to provide voluntary personnel for the local ambulance service and 'to care for the sick and suffering'.

In this photograph, taken in the St John's Hall, situated in Nether Row, members of the Thetford Brigade surround Divisional Superintendent E. Roberts, seen holding the County Commissioners Cup presented to Thetford in 1975. Today, there is a St John Forest Badger Sett of 6-11 year olds and an Ambulance Cadet Division from 11 year old onwards. [Photograph courtesy of Eileen Roberts]

CROXTON ROAD, c.1910

Thetford's roads and streets have provided an ideal playground for generations of countless children. When this photograph was taken, marbles, spinning tops, iron or wooden hoops and catapults were popular play things with boys and girls. Certainly in the back streets, road traffic created few problems for children and rarely interrupted games. To-day, despite the hazard of motor vehicles and the provision of play areas, children can occasionally be seen playing real or imaginary games in the street.

ST MARY'S ROW, 1946

These young children were all born in the war years. Whilst playing happily in the road, they are probably blissfully unaware of the turmoil that had surrounded their young lives. These young people, now grown-up with families of their own, may be reminded something of their precious childhood when viewing photographs such as this. From left to right: Veronica King, Diana Haywood, Malcolm King, Anne Clarke and Carol Barker.

Before demolition in the early 1960s St Mary's Row was lined each side with small, flint cottages and houses standing under the shadow of, St Mary's Church. [Photogaph courtesy of Violet Clarke]

SAXON PLACE, 1952

Some war-time rationing was still in force when these children were born in the immediate post-war years, a period that brought about a 'baby boom'. Moreover, it was this generation that was amongst the first to fully benefit from a nationalised health service.

The author has a personal interest in this photograph as he is amongst the children - second from the left in the front-row. Others include John Reeve, Ronnie James, Richard Pilbrow, Ann Reeve and Mary Osborne.

When Saxon Place was built as temporary Council housing in 1950-51, it stood on the outskirts of the town and there were still plenty of fields and open spaces for children to play and roam.

CASTLE PARK, c.1910

At some time most young girls have delighted in dressing-up in fine clothes, very often their mothers'. These pretty, young maidens, clothed in their best dresses and bonnets decorated with garlands, celebrate May Day. The young girl in the foreground is most probably the May Queen and the others her maidens-in-waiting. The celebration of May Day, the first day of May, is believed to have its origins in the Roman festival of Flora, the goddess of flowers. We still celebrate May Day with fêtes and carnivals, and occasionally school girls regale themselves with flowers.

CASTLE PARK, c.1925

Ever since the Castle meadow and ramparts was created a public park in September 1908, it has been a perfect haven for children to play and perhaps escape from parental control. Many Thetfordians will have childhood memories of playing hide-and-seek, impromptu games of football, cricket and rounders or perhaps scrambling up the side of the Castle Hill and sliding back down, oblivious to the damage inflicted on clothing and footwear.

MOTHER & TODDLER CLUB, 1996

Desipte the many social changes in recent years, the most natural of human bonds is that between a child and its mother.

In this photograph taken in the Methodist Church Hall, little Coral Richards, Katie McDermott and Lauren Robb share with their mothers, the love and joy of each others company in those precious formative years of childhood.

BOUGHTON'S PHOTOGRAPHIC STUDIO, 1917

How children's clothing fashions have changed since five year old John Osborne, his twin sister Gwendoline and elder sister Maud, posed in their 'Sunday best' for the photographer. The photograph was to be a keep-sake for their father, who, like many other men at that time, was fighting on the battlefields of France and Belgium. Unlike many children, these little innocents were able to welcome home the safe return of their father, unscathed from the horrific warfare.

NORWICH ROAD COUNTY COUNCIL SCHOOL, c.1917

School is also an important and memorable part of childhood. Even if some lessons are forgotten, teachers' names and faces often become eternally imprinted on our minds. Likewise, the threads of friendship formed in our schooldays can remain unbroken and with us for just as long.

At the very beginning of the 20th century, the Norwich Road School was known as the Board School, for it was originally governed by the Thetford School Board. The year following the 1902 Education Act, the school became the responsibility of Norfolk County Council.

Until January 1961 when Thetford Secondary Modern School opened, the majority of Thetford's children were educated at the Norwich Road School.

NORWICH ROAD COUNTY COUNCIL SCHOOL, 1925

These boys finished their school days to begin their working lives at the tender age of 14 years. It was not until 1947 that the school leaving age was advanced to 15 years and to 16 years in 1973.

Front row, left-right: -?-, G. Shaw, G. Webb, J. Parish, P. Crick, -?-, P. Ward, L. Page, Stagg, J. Osborne.
2nd row: Palmer, -?-, E. Jermy, -?-, Backlog, W. Petch, F. Miller, -?-, -?-, R. Carter, A. Secker.
3rd row: -?-, -?-, J. Kybird, -?-, R. Squires, A. Robinson, A. Sparrow, P. Rackham, W. Budd, -?-.
Back row: J. Barnard, -?-, -?-, G. Sharpe, -?-, -?-, -?-, M. Frost, F. Goddard.

NORWICH ROAD COUNTY COUNCIL SCHOOL, 1925

Like the boys, these girls also left school at the age of 14 years. At least four girls in this photograph went on to Thetford Girls' Grammar School and one eventually became a head teacher. One or two went into nursing or secretarial work but most of the others could find employment only in local shops or domestic service. Those in domestic service were sometimes many miles from home, very often the only employment opportunity for many working-class girls in the 1920s and 30s. Note the girls' boots that are once again fashionable today.

Front row, left-right: D. Mote, Sherwood, I. Lane, Reeve, Brett, C. Salter, G. Osborne, -?-, -?-.
2nd row: Hopkins, I. Langley, -?-, Sherwood, Reeve, N. Horwood, E. Flint, Crick, Makins, -?-, H. Ducker, Brett.
3rd row: -?-, M. Keymer, A. Lane, -?-, E. Manning, Reeve, S. Langford, M.Osborne, D. Chifney.
4th row: P. Cowls, Plummer, -?-, -?-, S. Foulger, D. Tate, K. Clarke, A. Gee, I. Hammond.

NORWICH ROAD COUNTY COUNCIL SCHOOL, 1949

The Norwich Road School was divided into three: Infants' School, Girls' School and Boys' School. The girls in this photograph were all about ten years old. The following year, after they had sat the 11-plus examination, a few girls were offered places at Thetford Grammar School. The 11-plus examination was introduced after the 1944 Education Act. The teacher standing on the left is Mrs Morris. Other teachers at the Girls' School at this time included Mrs Broom [Head], Mrs Christopher, Miss Minett, Miss Spinks, Miss Trett and Mrs Wright.

In the background is Thetford Police Station which was newly built and opened in 1936. A new station was built adjoining the old station in 1964, extended in 1971 and again in 1994. [Photograph courtesy of Norma Howard]

NORWICH ROAD COUNTY COUNCIL SCHOOL, 1955

Like several generations of boys before and after, these boys marched each week during the school term from the Norwich Road to the 'Rec' for their cricket or football matches. These young footballers won three shields in the 1954-55 season. The Senior team won the South Norfolk Knock-out competition for the second year running; the Under 14 team won the South Norfolk Knock-out competition and the Juniors the Runners-up Shield in the Junior South Norfolk Shield competition.

Front row, left-right: J. Salisbury, P. Squires, T. Ellis, D. Vincent, P. Goodwin, C. Fayers, E. Shepherd, R. Scott, Crawford, W. Filby. Centre row: I. Sayer, T. Blades, A. Cann, G. Angus, M. Parish, S. Rodwell, Mr D. Chamberlain [games master], M. Oulds, R. Mikalic, N. Wright, D. Wing, R. Brown. Back row: J. Balaam, T. Lee, A. Woods, G. Connochie, R. Thompson, G. Filby. [Photograph courtesy of Robert Thompson]

THETFORD SECONDARY MODERN SCHOOL, 1964

The first new school to be built in 20th century Thetford was the Queensway Infants' School in 1955. This was to cater for the growing population of young children in this part of the town. Four years later as families from London began settling on the new housing estates close to the Queensway school, building workers began constructing Thetford Secondary Modern School, on a thirteen acre site off Staniforth Road. In January 1961, exactly two years after building work began, the first Headmaster, Mr D. W. Briggs, welcomed about two-hundred and fifty children to the new school. Most of these new pupils had been transferred from the over-crowded Norwich Road School. The new Secondary Modern offered spacious, modern facilities and a different method of schooling. It was a striking contrast to the old Norwich Road school.

The school choir rehearses in the school foyer. These children are from a mixture of different backgrounds: old established Thetford families, families from the surrounding villages and new settlers from London and elsewhere. Throughout the 1960s and early 70s, hardly a week went by without the arrival of new pupils at Thetford's schools. [Photograph courtesy of Wendy Serjeant]

ABBEY FARM MIDDLE SCHOOL, 1993

It's computer time. Two young pupils are absorbed with the images they have helped to create using computer technology, an important part of today's school curriculum. It is a scene far removed from that of just a generation earlier.

Since the opening of Thetford Secondary Modern School (later renamed the Staniforth School and in 1982 the Charles Burrell High School) eight other new schools have opened in the town: Abbey Farm Middle - 1970; Admirals Middle - 1978; Canterbury Way First - 1970; Drake First- 1978; Elm Road Infants - 1970; Raleigh First - 1970; Red Castle Furze First & Middle - 1968 and Rosemary Musker High School - 1983. Some of these schools have changed status since and Elm Road is now closed. [Photograph courtesy of Dominic Cragoe, Headmaster of Abbey Farm School]

KING STREET, 1984

Children have often sought some kind of part-time employment as a source for providing pocket money and a sense of independence. This process is likely to begin within the family household, helping with household chores. Once the 'teenage' years arrive, children can be found before or after school hours and during school holidays, engaged in all sorts of jobs and chores, delivering newspapers, leaflets or groceries, running errands, washing cars and even looking after younger children.

A common sight in the main streets of Thetford on Saturdays, certainly since the 1980s, is that of children carrying sandwich-boards advertising local shops and services.

LINCOLN WAY, 1995

These happy, young children are taking part in a street party to celebrate the fiftieth anniversary of the allied forces Victory in Europe - VE Day. On Monday 8th May 1995, celebrations and events were held all over the country, acknowledging and remembering this historic event and the sacrifices made in the 1939-45 War. Other celebrations in Thetford included a concert by the RAF Honington Band in the Carnegie Room, a flower festival 'VE Day Remembered' in the Methodist Church and numerous parties scattered about the town. [Photograph courtesy of Eastern Counties Newspapers]

IN DEFENCE OF THE REALM

'1914 - 1918'

In ever grateful remembrance of the men of this borough who gave their lives in the Great War

"Lest We Forget"

1939 - 45

Inscribed on Thetford's War Memorial

THE MARKET PLACE, 1910

The men of Thetford who enlisted as part-time soldiers, in the early years of the 20th century, formed 'G' Company of the 4th Norfolk Rifle Volunteers. There was hardly a civic ceremony in the town without the presence of the Volunteers and they could often be seen marching about the town as they drilled and trained for warfare. This photograph of the local militia was taken in May 1910 for the Proclamation of King George V.

THETFORD CAMP, 1911

After the calamities of the Boer War, the Army was eventually reorganised. The old yeomanry and volunteer regiments were disbanded and a new Territorial Army formed in 1908.

The open Breckland landscape surrounding Thetford was considered ideal terrain for training the new army. In August 1911 special troop-trains transported between eight and nine thousand Territorials to Thetford for two weeks' training and manoeuvres. Hundreds of canvas tents were erected west of the town on Warren Heath.

THETFORD CAMP, 1911

A corrugated-iron building served as the Thetford Camp bakery for the duration of the exercise. The army was self-sufficient for most provisions, although Bidwell's Brewery are known to have supplied at least one ration of beer to the thirsty troops.

DOWN IN OUR THETFORD CAMP
To the tune of 'Back Home In Tennessee'.

I'm so lonely, oh, so lonely,
In our Blinking Camp,
I'm like a bloomin' tramp,
Not worth a penny stamp,
Father, Mother, Sister, Brother,
All are waiting me,
I'm getting thinner, miss my dinner
And my Sunday's tea.

CHORUS

Down in our Muddy Camp,
We're always on the ramp,
That's where we cop the cramp,
Through sleeping in the damp,
All we can hear each day,
Is Left...Right...march away.
Sergeants calling, Lance-jacks bawling
"Get out on parade".
We go to bed at night,
It is a glorious sight,
The earwigs on the floor,
Double-up and Form Fours.
Then when daylight is dawning,
You can hear our Sergeants yawnin'
Show-a-leg there. Show-a-leg there.
Down in our Thetford Camp.

From a postcard published c.1912

THETFORD CAMP, 1911

Troops march along Brandon Road towards the railway station on their return journey home. Extra railway staff were called into Thetford to deal with the operation of transporting nine thousand troops, five hundred horses and all their equipment on thirty special troop trains. All this had to be done without interrupting the normal rail service.

THETFORD CAMP, 1912

In September 1912, it was the turn of the regular forces to participate in another, but much larger exercise. About thirty thousand troops were deployed across East Anglia, including the countryside around Thetford. Lieutenant-General Sir Douglas Haig set-up his headquarters close to the Abbey Farm, and at Snarehill, in a field just off the Euston Road, a squadron of aeroplanes belonging to the newly formed Royal Flying Corps attracted the curiosity of hundreds of spectators, including Thetford photographer, Roger Bantock.

THE 4TH NORTHAMPTONS, 1914

As the troops returned to their barracks and homes from the dry, sandy Breckland after the manoeuvres in 1911 and 1912 they could not have foreseen that many of them would soon be fighting and dying on the muddy battlefields of Flanders or in the distant Dardenelles.

War against Germany was declared on August 4th 1914. Within hours, Thetford's territorials were mobilised. Soon afterwards, other men from the town volunteered for military service. By November 1914, Thetford had once again taken on the appearance of a military garrison as the 4th Northampton Regiment became the first of many units to be billeted in the town, amongst the homes of rich and poor alike.

BURRELL MUNITIONS WORKERS, 1917

In 1915, as the number of khaki-clad soldiers in the town increased, a tented army camp was erected near Barnham Cross Common and in the following year huts were erected at a more permanent camp built just off the London Road. Late in 1915 the Royal Flying Corps reassembled their aerodrome at Snarehill, although on a different site.

After conscription was introduced in 1916 the town's industries and businesses recruited women and girls to replace the men who had enlisted into the armed forces. Production of traction engines at the Burrell works almost ceased as the manufacture of munitions, employing large numbers of women working in shifts, took priority. [Photograph courtesy of Garry Burrell]

FLORRIE CLARKE, c.1917

Many Thetfordians, besides those serving in the armed forces, made some contribution to the war effort. Thetford's old veteran soldiers formed a Volunteer Training Corps and Boy Scouts zealously guarded telegraph lines against tampering by enemy agents! Besides munitions work, women were also employed as administrators and Red Cross nurses. Volunteers busily knitted garments for the troops from their Guildhall HQ. While John Clarke was away on military service, his daughter Florrie took on his duties as Town Crier and Billposter. [Photograph courtesy of Mary Hayes]

'BOOM' WEEK, 1918

This gentleman, photographed outside W. Boughton's Station Road printing works, toured the town with his pony and cart, encouraging people to invest in National War Bonds. Thetford's 'Boom' or Tank Week, held in May 1918, raised over £57,000 in war bonds and savings certificates.

CASTLE PARK, 1919

After the war many of the nation's cities and towns were given a captured German artillery piece as some kind of souvenir. This gun was displayed in the Castle Park from 1919 until 1928 when it was sold for scrap, although components of any scrap value had disappeared long before then.

THE MARKET PLACE, PEACE DAY, 1919

The hostilities ceased at 11 o'clock on the 11th November 1918 a few hours after an armistice was agreed between the warring nations. It ended four long years of hardship and grief. When the news of peace reached Thetford about mid-day, it was greeted with great excitement. The church bells rang as soldiers, munitions workers and Thetfordians linked arms and paraded the town. On the Market Place, Florrie Clarke, Thetford's Town Crier, proclaimed the peace.

On the 19th July 1919, the nation officially celebrated peace. In this view on the Market Place, Mr G. Hayes conducts a united choir, accompanied by the band of the 2nd Norfolks. A wreath bearing the words 'Lest We Forget' was hung on the old market pump.

In a marquee in the Abbey grounds, about four hundred and fifty of Thetford's demobilised servicemen were given a luncheon. This was followed by an 'Olde English Fete', a river carnival, music concert and a bonfire on the Warren Heath where so many soldiers had trained for war just a few years earlier.

THETFORD OLD COMRADES BAND, c.1920

Within a few months of the war ending, thousands of troops had once again passed through Thetford Camp, the demobilisation centre for all soldiers living in Norfolk, Suffolk and Cambridgeshire. Once they had received their 'demob' suits or two pounds twelve shillings and six pence [£2. 62½p.] in lieu of the suit [most took the money] and returned to their homes and civilian life, there was little military activity in the town for another two decades.

Thetford's demobilised servicemen soon formed their associations, parading the town with their flags and medals at least once a year to commemorate Armistice Day and honour those who had made the supreme sacrifice. This photograph taken on the Market Place is one such occasion with music provided by the Old Comrades Band, a group of ex-servicemen led by bandmaster Harold Bowes.

THE MARKET PLACE, 1921

Hundreds of Thetfordians crowded the Market Place for the unveiling of the War Memorial – 4th December, 1921. The memorial was erected by public subscription. *In ever grateful remembrance of the men of this borough who gave their lives in the Great War "Lest We Forget".*

It is probable that between 600-700 Thetford men [about 15% of the population] served in the armed forces during the Great War. Of these men, 116 were killed. A further 43 names were added to Thetford's War Memorial in memory of those killed in the 1939-1945 War.

EX-SERVICEMEN'S CLUB, c.1930

Immediately after the Great War many of Thetford's demobilised soldiers found themselves unemployed. It was organisations such as Thetford's Ex-Servicemen's Club, formed in 1920, that offered comradeship and hope. The following year they purchased a number of wooden army huts when the Thetford Camp was dismantled. These huts were erected as club rooms on a piece of land acquired just off Mill Lane. A new brick-built club room was erected on the site in 1952 and the old huts demolished a few years later.

One old Thetford Camp hut still survives in the town today. It is a private residence in the Bury Road known as 'The Haven'.

YOU CAN SEE THE CAR
WHEN THE DRIVER
CAN'T SEE YOU

LOOK OUT
IN THE BLACKOUT!

EVACUEES ARRIVE AT THETFORD, 1939

By the mid-1930s, as the signs of another European war increased, Thetford's part-time military force had been reorganised as the Thetford Detachment 250th Field Company Royal Engineers [TA] based in Minstergate. Thetford Borough Council was also kept busy implementing the Air Raid Precautions Act, 1937. Air Raid Wardens, Auxiliary Firemen, Civil Defence Volunteers and other emergency services were recruited and organised.

Even before the Prime Minister's historic broadcast at 11 o'clock on Sunday 3rd September 1939 announcing, *'this country is at war with Germany'*, the first evacuees from London had already arrived in the town. Within a few days over 2,000 evacuees, mostly children and mothers with young babies, had been housed in Thetford and the surrounding district. [Photograph courtesy of Eastern Counties Newspapers]

THE GUILDHALL, c.1940

After the events of September 1939 ‘normal life’ took on a different meaning. Britain was once again at war and there were so many new rules and regulations to obey, from instructions on how to deal with incendiary bombs, the wearing of gas masks, rationing restrictions, identity cards and the stringent Lighting Restrictions Act.

Men and women from Thetford were enlisted or conscripted into the armed forces and other organisations such as the Women’s Land Army. Once again, Thetford became crowded with soldiers and airmen while Thetford’s civilian population involved themselves in the war effort in all sorts of different ways. These ladies are members of the WVS knitters organised by the Mayoress, Mrs Florence Lambert, making knitted garments for the troops. [Photograph courtesy of the Ancient House Museum].

WATCH YOUR MEAT COUPONS
These can be Accepted by
GEO. REEVE Pork Butcher, THETFORD
Coupons already deposited with a general butcher may be retreived for such use. Sauges, Fry, Kidneys and Pork Cheeses can be obtained without coupons.

THE MARKET PLACE, 1940

Members of Thetford Women’s Voluntary Service, the WVS, on duty at a scrap metal stall set-up inside the Shambles, July 1940. This was just after the Battle of Britain and was part of a government scheme to turn aluminium saucepans into aeroplanes. About the same time many of the decorative cast-iron railings that adorned properties in the town were dismantled and removed for scrap. Another casualty was the cast-iron Market Pump, much regaled at the end of the Great War just twenty years earlier.

The WVS played an important role throughout the war, organising evacuees, canteens for the troops and such tasks as instructing housewives how to cook with the minimum of ingredients. [Photograph courtesy of Eastern Counties Newspapers]

No.3 SECTION, 288 FIELD COMPANY ROYAL ENGINEERS, 1940

On Friday 1st September 1939, Thetford's Territorials - 251 Field Park Company RE [TA], formerly 250th Field Company - a unit of about 60 men from Thetford, Brandon and district, were ordered to report to their Minstergate HQ. The following day they travelled to Norwich where they joined other Engineer TA units. Most of the Thetford and Brandon men were posted to 288 Field Company. After carrying out duties at nearby Weeting Hall, West Tofts and Cranwich they found themselves at Haveringland Hall, 10 miles north of Norwich, where this photograph was taken. After working on military defences along the north Norfolk coast early in 1940 they embarked at Liverpool docks the following year, bound for Nova Scotia.

Early in 1942 they eventually arrived in Singapore, just a few weeks before the island was invaded and captured by the Japanese forces. Not all of Thetford's 'sappers' survived the Japanese POW and work camps, but those who did were thankful to return to their families and native town. Included in this photograph: Sid Butters, Fred Howell, Jimmy James, Ronnie Knights, Richard Nutt, Cyril Pearson, Ted Secker, Ken Spinks and Peter Starling all of Thetford. Stanley Steward of Barnham, Bernard Bidwell and Clarence Carey of Fakenham Magna, Melvin Rushbrooke of Honington and 'Snowy' Davis of Rushford. [Photograph courtesy of Peter Starling].

THETFORD RAILWAY STATION, c.1941

Tanks of the 5th Royal Irish Dragoon Guards 9th Armoured Division entrain at the railway station after a large-scale exercise in the area. It was in the 1914-18 War that the very first tank crews were trained at a top secret site located between the nearby villages of Barnham and Elveden. [Photograph courtesy of The Trustees of the Imperial War Museum, London]

BELL CORNER, 1941

As children make their way to school, a Mk.1 Valentine tank roars around the Bell Corner into Bridge Street. It was part of a large-scale anti-invasion exercise that took place in the Thetford and Barton Mills area during April 1941. The Thetford area was used extensively for troop training throughout the war. Camouflaged tanks, bren-gun carriers and other military vehicles were often concealed in the local countryside for long periods while on manoeuvres. Moreover, airfields, army camps and other permanent military sites were established nearby. [Photograph courtesy of the Trustees of the Imperial War Museum, London]

SOLDIERS HARVESTING THE CROPS, 1942

In 1942, several parishes and villages just to the north of Thetford were evacuated to make way for a Battle School, a large area of the countryside, out-of-bounds to the general public, where soldiers could be trained in war-like conditions. In the autumn of 1942 over 1,000 troops were engaged harvesting sugar beet, potatoes and other root crops left behind by the evacuated farmers. In this photograph, taken near Thetford, soldiers are pulling sugar beet. [Photograph courtesy of the Trustees of the Imperial War Museum, London]

YMCA c.1942

With so many allied troops and airmen of different nationalities stationed in the district, Thetford's cafés, pubs and other social centres were often packed with off-duty servicemen. The YMCA in Magdalen Street was used as a canteen for HM Forces and civilian Civil Defence personnel.

In this photograph a Church Army mobile canteen is being loaded with fresh provisions before visiting troops in the training areas. [Photograph courtesy of Brian Carr]

GUILDHALL, c.1942

Soldiers in battledress, uniformed airmen and local young people smile for the photographer at one of the regular dances held in the Guildhall during the dark days of war. Occasions such as this were essential in helping to keep a high morale and spirits when so many young lives were put into turmoil and danger.

In 1942 after the so-called 'friendly invasion' of American forces, who were stationed in large numbers in the neighbourhood, dances held on the American camps and bases soon proved to be popular events with local girls in particular. [Photograph courtesy of Pat Boughen]

THETFORD OBSERVER CORPS POST, c.1938

The Observer Corps was another organisation whose members performed valuable war work. The role of the Observer Corps was aircraft tracking and reporting. The Thetford Post belonged to No. 14 Group, Bury St Edmunds and was one of many hundreds positioned every ten miles throughout the United Kingdom. Thetford's Post was sited on the edge of Barnham Cross Common, close to where Queensway is today, and consisted of a telephone pole to which a standard army issue head-set could be connected for communication with Headquarters. Later, a shelter was also provided.

Members of the Corps were local people from all walks of life who were chosen for their good character and eyesight but were too old or young for military service. The Corps was called out on 29 August 1939 and all Posts and Headquarters were manned continuously for five and a half years. Such was the importance of the Corps during the Battle of Britain, King George VI granted the Corps permission to use the title 'Royal' in April 1941.

Back row, left-right: S. Gooch, D. Doran, F. O'Nians, G. Bacon, A. Green, M. Lambert, B. Gould, F. Bell, Police Inspector Dye, R. Reeve.

Centre row: A. Hallum, Carter, H. Earl, P. Jackson, Elwood, C. Saunders, F. Potter, A. Hansord.

Front: G. Boughton, J. Munns.

THETFORD HOME GUARD, c.1945

A Local Defence Volunteers force of men between the ages of 17 and 65 years, who were *'capable of free movement'*, was formed nationally in 1940 but was soon renamed the Home Guard. The Thetford unit, part of 'C' Company 8th Norfolk Home Guard, was formed about May 1940. The Thetford HQ was at Bridge House the home of the commanding officer, Major E.G. Wilton. Besides regular training sessions, each night members of the Home Guard patrolled such strategic places as the railway station, post office, water works and petrol dump.

In the late-1960s and early 1970s uniformed soldiers of the Home Guard were once again seen in the streets of Thetford, when episodes of the popular BBC television programme 'Dad's Army' were filmed in the town. [Photograph courtesy of Nessie Horwood]

THETFORD ARP WARDENS, VE DAY 1945

These men and women are amongst those who acted as Thetford's Air Raid Precautions Wardens during the 1939-45 War. They were photographed just before finally standing down on VE Day 8th May 1945. The ARP headquarters were located in the Guildhall.

Back row, left-right: -?-, H. Johnson, J. Barnet, -?-, A. Parry, A. Sponcer, -?-, C. Watson, R. Cates, -?-, E. Bowes, G. Bacon, F. Boggis, Gould, A. Mayes, -?-.

Centre row: I. Ashby, J. Woods, F. Steele, -?-, A. Mills, -?-, -?-, E. Page, Roberts, S. Cook, -?-, T. Clarke, R. Pert, -?-, -?-, T. Skoyles.

Front row: L. Tromans, B. Palmer, M. Scott, W. Hitchcock, E. Pert, G. Large, H. Leech, J.Fraser, Miss Edwards, D. Steele, W. Hiller, G. Gooch.

THETFORD ARMY CADET FORCE, 1995

Although the ACF dates back to the 19th century, it was the mid-1960s before a unit of the ACF was formed in Thetford with its HQ in the old British Legion building in White Hart Street [now Wereham House]. The ACF moved to a purpose-built centre at Thetford Secondary Modern School in the late 1960s before moving to their Croxton Road HQ in 1992. The Croxton Road Cadet Training Centre was officially opened in December 1992 by Lt. Gen. Sir David Scott-Barrett KBE MC.

Boys and girls aged between 13 and 18 years are eligible to join the ACF whose aim is to inspire young people to achieve success in life with a spirit of service to the Queen, country, local community, and to develop the qualities required of a good citizen. One of the annual duties performed by the local Cadet Force is the cleaning of the War Memorial prior to the Remembrance Service.

This photograph was taken as the Cadets parade along King Street, having taken part in the annual Remembrance Service on the Market Place.

REMEMBRANCE PARADE, c.1950

In this photograph Thetford Borough Band leads the British Legion and other local organisations along Castle Street towards the Market Place. The Borough Band was formed in 1946 by Hector Sutherland and Ben Culey. When this photograph was taken, members of the band included: B. Smith, Drum-major; V. Clarke, O. Ladell, bass; P. Bowes, C. Friend, trombone; Dr. O. Bewers, euphonium; T. Bidwell, A. Large, H. Scott, tenor horn; H. Bowes, B. Carr, R. McCreedy, I. Rickwood, H. Sutherland, cornet; S. Chase, G. Kybird, G. Stiff, percussion. [Photograph courtesy of Peter Bowes]

REMEMBRANCE PARADE, MARKET PLACE, 1995

Each year since 1919, there has been an Armistice parade and service to honour and remember those Thetfordians who sacrificed their lives in the defence of our nation. This annual event is organised each year by the local branch of the Royal British Legion.

Earlier in the century the whole nation would stand, patriotically in silence, at the eleventh hour of the eleventh day of the eleventh month, no matter what day of the week it fell. This practice was revived at 11 o'clock on Saturday 11th November 1995, the day previous to this service, when the local Royal British Legion lowered their Colours at the War Memorial while many in the town stopped their busy activities, to stand in silence for two minutes in remembrance of all those men and women who have given us our freedom by serving the nation, not only in the two world wars, but in the many other conflicts.

WHERE WE SHOPPED

'This used to be a thriving little market town. When I came here in the 60s you could not move. Now shops are pulling out. There are only the charity shops which don't really attract people in and are subsided by our rates'.
Thetford Chamber of Trade Chairman, Bryan Leonard discussing the threat facing Thetford's town centre, following the proposal to build another out-of-town supermarket.
Published Eastern Daily Press, 27 February 1995.

TANNER STREET, c.1910

In the early years of the century, itinerant traders continued the ancient custom of hawking or peddling a wide-range of goods and services about the streets of the town. In this photograph, fruit and vegetables are peddled from a barrow. Modern door-to-door peddlers are more likely to offer insurance and finance services or double glazing.

These cottages were demolished in the late 1960s and the site is now occupied by a turf accountant.

THE MARKET PLACE, c.1925

From photographs such as this, it would seem that in the early years of the century, Thetford's Saturday market was never much larger than five or six stalls, selling fruit, vegetables, eggs, fish and small wares.

Thetford's Saturday market is an ancient privilege, while the Tuesday market is a recent development, having been established in 1970. Before then, a few traders held a weekday market on Wednesdays but this appears not to have been an old practice.

THE MARKET PLACE, 1924

Market trader, Arthur Holmes, poses in front of his fruit and vegetable stall. On the right stands his wife Anna and daughter Daisy. Many people will have memories of Daisy playing the organ at St Cuthbert's and St Peter's Church for many years. [Photograph courtesy of the Ancient House Museum]

THE MARKET PLACE, 1996

Thetford's Saturday market on a bright morning in April. Today there are about 30 stalls selling a great variety of goods: fruit, vegetables, fish, meat, confectionery, flowers and plants, clothing, books, jewellery and all manner of household goods. Market traders travel to Thetford from all over the district and some have been attending Thetford's Market Place for many years. The late Sidney 'Pinky' Wright, who traded on the Market Place from the mid-1940s into the early 1970s is fondly remembered by many. Since the construction of the Carnegie Room, market stalls now extend along part of Well Street, providing space for a total of about forty-eight stalls.

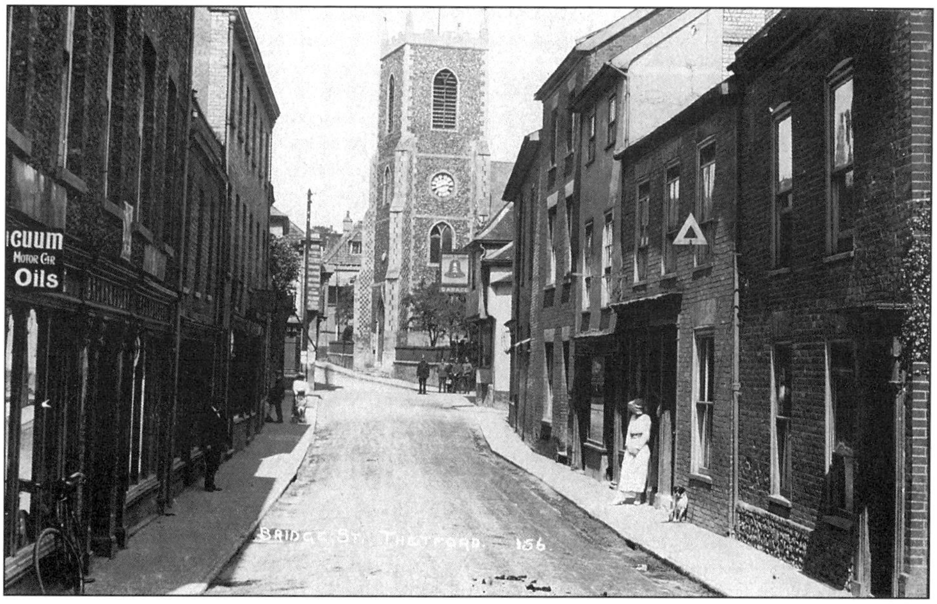

BRIDGE STREET, c.1910

As the town's main thoroughfare until the late 1960s, Bridge Street and White Hart Street have been lined with shops and other commercial premises for centuries. When this photograph was taken, ironmongers Brown & Colby traded from the premises in the left foreground, now occupied by Witton and Studio Five. Opposite at number 5 was George Ball's bakery and confectionery shop, later taken over by W. H. Young. All of the premises on the right were demolished in the early 1960s to make way for the Bell Hotel extension.

Other Bridge Street traders at different times in the 20th century have been: W. Huggins, butcher; J. Marshall, tobacconist; E. & D. Payne, tobacconist; B. Pett, men's outfitter; Suzanne's, ladies hairdresser. Estate agent Witton, and Graham Jacob's photographic shop 'Studio Five' are old established Bridge Street businesses still trading today. However, the oldest established business in Bridge Street today is Barclay's Bank. [Photograph courtesy of John 'Charlie' Leeder]

BRIDGE STREET, c.1925

Master saddler, Thomas Beckett, began trading from this shop at 8, Bridge Street in 1920 and continued there until 1932 when he moved his business and family to Warwickshire. As can be seen from this interesting photograph, a wide range of goods was offered for sale. Many of the leather wares on display were made or fashioned on the premises in a back-room workshop, a tradition that was already rapidly disappearing. Note the sign advertising Standard fireworks. Beckett's ran a fireworks club that boys could pay into each week, before collecting their fireworks on the 5th November. Many other shopkeepers ran similar schemes, to help people provide extra provisions needed for special occasions, particularly Christmas.

Number 8, Bridge Street continued as a saddlers shop until 1944. For many years afterwards it was a ladies' hairdressing salon and is now an estate agents. [Photograph courtesy of Constance Mary Beckett]

BRIDGE STREET, c.1925

Tom Gunstone's refreshment and sweet shop at 17, Bridge Street was conveniently situated close to the two grammar schools. By 1931, Gunstone's shop had become known as the Corner House Tea Rooms [proprietress E. Hazell], advertising luncheons, teas, high-class confectionery and tobacco. In the early 1970s The Corner House, as it was then known, was still serving luncheons and teas. Soon afterwards it was refurbished as a Chinese restaurant.

WHITE HART STREET, 1974

Ben Palmer began in the grocery business as an apprentice at Thetford's Savage Bros and then the International Stores. In 1932 Ben Palmer and his brother George, who had also begun learning the grocery trade with the International Stores, took over an empty shop at 1, White Hart Street and continued trading from there until closure and retirement in April 1974.

From 1923 until 1970, the shop on the opposite corner in Bridge Street, was occupied by Mr Bernard Pett's gents' clothing and ladies' hosiery business. Earlier in the century Bernard's father, Thomas Pett, sold clothing from the premises later occupied by Palmer's Stores at 1, White Hart Street. [Photograph courtesy of Rita Christian]

WHITE HART STREET, c.1920

After Thomas Potter moved from Essex to Thetford at the end of the 19th century, his son Frederick W. E. Potter, along with Edward Moss of Swaffham, began trading as wine merchants Moss & Potter, with premises at Brandon, Mildenhall, Watton and Thetford.

In this photograph Frederick Potter stands outside his shop at 11, White Hart Street. Moss & Potter Ltd, also owned the St Nicholas Brewery Stores or 'London' public house in St Nicholas Street. Next-door to the 'London' was Moss & Potter's bottling department where beers, wines, spirits and minerals were bottled and labelled with the firm's own brand labels.

Moss & Potter Ltd were taken over by Hunter & Oliver Ltd in 1957 and since the early 1970s their former premises in White Hart Street have been occupied by Thetford Typewriter Services. [Photograph courtesy of Richard Potter]

KING STREET, c.1910

King Street continues as Thetford's principle high street, even though the Riverside Walk shopping precinct was opened in the late 1960s. With the passing of time, new shops have come and gone. Very few of today's shopkeepers were trading in the town more than forty years ago. Moreover, it is a completely different shopping scene, dictated by the market economy. The size and appearance of both the shop-front and interior has changed, as have the goods and services that are offered.

When this photograph was taken, most shops were family businesses. On the left can be seen Mr Starling's barber shop. The large building beyond was Palmer's bakery and refreshment rooms. Opposite is the chemist shop of H. J. Bromhall and boot and shoemakers Gooch & Son. One of King Street's largest and best remembered shops is that of Savage Bros.

KING STREET, c.1910

Thetford's first multi-national store was probably a branch of the International Tea Company that opened in the mid-1890s at 13, White Hart Street. By the time that this photograph was taken, the International had moved to this shop in King Street [now the Trustee Savings Bank]. Each branch of the International was easily recognisable by its shop-front, duplicated at International Stores across the country, a trend that has been vigorously pursued in the high street by later multi-nationals.

International Stores later moved into the Riverside Walk premises of Pricerite Ltd who opened there in 1968. The premises are now occupied by Argos.

KING STREET, c.1925

Late in the 19th century Robert Carley's printing and bookselling premises were taken over by J. W. Clarke. J. W. Clarke's son was William G. Clarke [1877-1925] the celebrated local historian, naturalist and author of *'In Breckland Wilds'* and numerous Thetford Town Guides. Clarke's ancient premises, now occupied by T & W Wines, was a popular shop for newspapers, stationery, toys, fishing tackle and fancy goods until closure in the late 1960s.

KING STREET, c.1925

Savage Bros began trading from King Street in 1905 when Mr A. J. Savage acquired Henry Webster's shop. Savage Bros gradually expanded their shop premises and vied with the Thetford Co-op as the town's premier emporium, although some might have argued that Savage's was of a better class.

In the 1950s, Savages advertised: *'The Best Quality, Style and Service in Groceries, Provisions, Wines & Spirits, Ladies' Gentlemen's and Children's Outfitting, Drapery, Furniture, etc'*.

In November 1961, it was announced that Messrs Savage Bros had been acquired by a London development company. Savages pulled the shutters down for the last time early in 1962. Soon afterwards the old fashioned but much loved shop was demolished and replaced by new but less endearing, retail premises.

SAVAGE BROS.
Warehousemen
2·4&6·KING ST·THETFORD

KING STREET, 1996

It's early Saturday morning as shoppers begin to make their appearance. Soon, the pavement will be much more crowded on this traditional shopping day.

The modern shops on the left, occupied by Superdrug and the Halifax Building Society, stand on the site of Savage's old emporium. Green's old newspaper and stationery shop is now occupied by the British Heart Foundation [also see page 21]. The adjacent premises, once Parry & Large and now occupied by Lloyds, have been a chemists shop since the last century. Opposite Lloyds is the Keymarket supermarket, opened in 1971.

KING STREET, c.1905

The premises from right-left: International Tea Company Stores Limited, grocers, W. Boughton & Sons Ltd, studio photographers and picture frame makers, Mulles & Bircham, boot and shoe makers, W. Hannant, hairdresser and tobacconist and the 'Chequers' public house.

The late Gertrude Minett, born in Thetford at the end of the 19th century, recalled her childhood memories, *'I Remember Thetford'* a series of articles published in 1971. *'Now that so many familiar landmarks are disappearing it is pleasant to recall the main streets even before the old shop fronts were modernised. Small and poky they may have been, with narrow steps leading up to small doorways and windows of square panes, and some of these were bowed and picturesque. They were of course, lit by oil lamps or gas brackets'...'We had more variety in the town in those days than we have now. There was the gunsmith's and the saddlers...two or three excellent butchers' shops and good class bakeries, also three good stores which could supply a great variety of goods. One of these had the grocery department on one side and the corset and haberdashery opposite'.*

KING STREET, c.1955

Certainly on occasions before the 1960s, Thetford's pavements may have been busy with shoppers but they were never crowded. Most of these premises have seen different shopkeepers come and go since the early years of the century and when this photograph was taken, the International stores is the one exception. Next-door to the International was Turner's shoe shop [formerly W. Boughton's photographic studio and shop], adjacent is Dewhurst the butchers [formerly the photographic studio and shop of R. J. Bantock], Mr & Mrs Baxter's ladies' and gents' hairdressing salon [formerly Broadhurst's hairdressing salon and before that Hannant's barber and tobacconists shop], H. W. Ellis' game, fruit and vegetable shop [formerly the Chequers public house and pork butcher's shop of publican Ephraim Knights; also see page 20]. [Photograph courtesy Studio Five, Thetford]

KING STREET, c.1963

Thetfordians were delighted with the opening of F. W. Woolworth's King Street store in 1961. It was the first big shop of its kind in the town and, in its way, gave Thetford some kind of commercial prestige. Later, F. W. Woolworth acquired the adjoining Walker's store, that had also opened in 1961. Woolworth's shop was completely refurbished in 1987 and 1996. The front of Adderley's bakery and tea rooms can just be seen on the left of the photograph. Before early 1971 when decimal currency was introduced, we went shopping with a pocket full of different coins. There was then twelve pennies to a shilling [5p] and twenty shillings to one pound sterling. [Photograph courtesy of Thetford Town Council]

KING STREET, 1984

Adderley's began trading from King Street in 1924, in the premises occupied earlier in the century by pastry cook, H. Palmer, *'The Best House for Light Refreshments'*. Adderley's continued Palmer's traditions of baking on the premises.

Adderley's tea rooms and bakery were a favourite retreat for shoppers. Indeed, there are many who must have fond memories of the warm aroma of Adderley's freshly baked bread and cakes, while sipping a cup of refreshing tea or coffee and resting from the rigours of shopping.

The bottom photograph was taken on a busy Saturday afternoon just one week before Adderley's finally closed in February 1984. Adderley's former premises have been refurbished and are now occupied by Martins the newsagent.

GUILDHALL STREET, c.1914

Bury St Edmunds seed merchant, E. E. Westgate, moved into these premises at 19, Guildhall Street in 1913. The business was taken over by F. W. Myhill in the mid-1950s and continued supplying seeds, animal foods and gardening tools and equipment until closure in 1993. Like Clarke's old shop in King Street, this is another very old building with a modern facade.

GUILDHALL STREET, c.1920

Herbert Ellis, fish and fruit merchant, and licensed game dealer, traded from this shop at 4, Guildhall Street, next-door to the Dog and Partridge public house, until 1922. The family business, established in the middle of the 19th century then moved to 42 King Street, part of the former Chequers public house and continued trading from there until 1962 when the building was demolished [see page 20].

Turkeys are in abundance in this photograph, which was obviously taken just before the Christmas festivities. A more common fare on local tables was pheasant or rabbit, found in abundance on the local heaths and estates. Rabbit meat, in particular, formed a substantial part of many local diets in the first half of the 20th century. Although there were several licensed game dealers in the town, poaching was a common, illegal pursuit amongst some sections of local society. [Photograph courtesy of the Ancient House Museum]

GUILDHALL STREET, c.1935

From humble beginnings in the middle of the 19th century, the Thetford Co-op had grown into the largest shop in Thetford before the beginning of the 20th century. This growth and expansion continued, so that by the early 1960s, the main store in Guildhall Street boasted eight large departments. There were also three branch stores in the town. Changes in 1971, however, created the Guildhall Street Co-op store into a large CRS [Co-operative Retail Services Ltd.] supermarket that finally ceased trading in 1987. The familiar facade of the old Co-op disappeared in 1989 when the site was cleared for redevelopment, a project that has as yet to proceed.

Undoubtedly many former shareholders of the Thetford Co-operative Society Ltd can still remember their old share (or cheque) number, which was quoted each time a purchase was made to qualify for a dividend. It was at the Co-op grocery department in 1956 that Thetfordians were introduced for the first time to a new trend in shopping - the American-style self-service store.

Included in this photograph: Mabel Kendall, Arthur Cowles, Jim Ollington, Wilf Snelling, Sam Root, Tom Skoyles, Charlie Everett and F. Tomlinson.

GUILDHALL STREET, 1989

Until the 1990s, there were always several small, hardware shops trading in the town centre. One by one they disappeared, unable to compete with the large multi-national DIY stores and builders' merchants established on the periphery of the town. One of the first traders on this site in Guildhall Street was Joseph Brighton, a former carpenter at the Burrell Works. From the early 1930s Brighton sold new and second-hand furniture, ironmongery and hardware from his shop. He also traded from a horse-drawn cart, travelling around the local villages. During the war, Brighton's turned their shop into a tea and refreshment room. Robert 'Bob' Carter, a local signwriter and decorator, took over the premises in 1959 and once again they were turned into a hardware store. Carter's premises were completely rebuilt in 1969 before closing in 1992 The premises are now a chicken bar and take-away.

ST NICHOLAS STREET, c.1910

When this photograph was taken, St Nicholas Street [formerly Back Street] was a vibrant community lined with houses, cottages and several commercial properties. There were certainly many more corner and back-street shops in the town, at least until the 1960s. The Back Street Co-op, as it was commonly known, was conveniently situated, supplying nearby residents with groceries and provisions from 1907 until closure in the mid-1960s. The old Co-op and adjoining properties were then demolished to provide a car park. In the early 1990s the car park was cleared for the construction of Breckland District Council's new office complex - 'Breckland House'.

ST NICHOLAS STREET, c.1920

Like many small shopkeepers in the first-half of the century, Albert Lockwood and his family lived above or behind the shop premises. Lockwood's confectionery and tea rooms stood on the corner of Minstergate and St Nicholas Street, close to the Burrell works. Opening hours began at 5.30 in the morning to cater for the Burrell workforce before they began their day at 6 o'clock and men who travelled out of the town for work each day.

Lockwood's premises were eventually taken over by Charlie Pearson and continued as a workmen's cafe until demolished in the mid-1960s.

ST NICHOLAS STREET, c.1935

Witting's little general store could be found at the top or north end of St Nicholas Street. After closure as a general store, it was the shop premises of Mr F. C. Witting, Thetford's last working saddler. Mr Witting retired from business in 1970. Although closed for many years, the shop-front is still recognisable, but alas, without those colourful, enamel advertising signs.

CASTLE STREET, 1975

Frank Clarke began trading as an ironmonger from 53 Castle Street in 1905. Three years later he moved across the road to this site at number 36. In 1931, Frank Clarke advertised gramophones and records, wireless sets, baby carriages, sporting guns and ammunition, cycles and accessories.

Clarke's family business changed hands in 1965 but continued trading under Clarke's name until the premises were severely damaged by fire in 1973. After the fire, other businesses traded from the site for a few more years. The building was demolished and eventually in 1991 Rampart Way, a new road linking Castle Street with Raymond Street was built through Clarke's old site.

EARLS STREET, c.1930

Specialist pork butcher, George Reeve, stands outside his Earls Street shop established in 1912. An appetising display of pork sausages fill the shop window. Other specialities included hams, bacon, lard, pork cheeses and dripping. After George Reeve's death in 1942 his shop was eventually taken over by his former assistant Mr Geoffrey Mitchell who, in turn, was succeeded by his son, Mervyn, until closure in 1994. The old butchers shop is now a hairdressing salon. [Photograph courtesy of Geoff 'Hippy' Wright]

BURY ROAD, c.1914

Once the area between the Bury Road and London Road began to be developed just before the Great War, the Thetford Co-operative Society built and opened this branch store, close by on the corner of Mill Lane in 1913. It continued as a branch store until closure in 1971 and now forms part of the premises of an upholstery business. When this photograph was taken the Thetford Co-op Society employed a total of 30 males and 7 females. Progress took place at the Bury Road branch store in 1927 when a mechanical bacon slicer was installed.

MINSTERGATE, 1992

Even before restrictions on Sunday trading were relaxed in 1994, Sunday markets and car boot sales, also usually held on a Sunday, were already a common sight at all sorts of local venues such as school playgrounds and the town's car parks. Although car boot sales began as a market for individuals to dispose of surplus or unwanted household or personal possessions, professional market traders can be found there.

This is a car boot sale held on the Gateway supermarket car park. Tommy Mapplebeck waits at the boot of his car for customers.

RIVERSIDE WALK, 1995

Since opening in 1968 there has been an almost continuous change of shops and shopkeepers trading from the Riverside Walk. Former traders include ironmongers Ben Foreman Ltd, TV and electrical supplier Sam Holden Ltd, discount goods retailer B. B. Adams, men's and boys' outfitter Waites, supermarket traders Fineware, International Stores, Tesco and Pricerite.

Acts of vandalism after shop closing hours has been a frequent problem in parts of the town centre, certainly since the late 1970s. Many traders have recently fitted protective shutters that completely obscure the window display when the shop is closed. As in other parts of the county, close-circuit television [CCTV] was installed in 1995 to monitor parts of the town centre. [Photograph courtesy of Carl Richards]

J. SAINSBURY'S SUPERMARKET, FOREST RETAIL PARK, 1991, 1995 & 1996

These huge, brightly-lit shopping palaces, appropriately known as supermarkets, are now found on the outskirts of many towns. They were undreamt of by most Thetfordians just a few decades ago. Indeed, who could have imagined that such a variety of provisions and goods could be so temptingly displayed under one roof?

Self service shopping arrived at Thetford in 1936 [see page 83] and afterwards a few small, self-service stores opened, such as Walker's Stores, and W. J. Adkins in King Street. From these modest establishments, Thetford's shoppers progressed in 1986 to Keymarket's new riverside store built in Minstergate on the site of the old fruit and vegetable canning factory. Five years later, Thetford's first out-of-town supermarket was opened by Tesco at Kilverstone, closely followed by J. Sainsbury at the Forest Retail Park on the opposite side of the town. [Interior photographs courtesy of J. Sainsbury and A.J. Allison]

HOME SWEET HOME

'The commonest type of house in the town is the four-roomed cottage with a yard behind, in which are situated the sanitary convenience - usually as far from the house as possible'.

From the Medical Officer of Health's report to the Thetford Urban District, December 1912

THE KING'S HOUSE, c.1938

Most towns have a rich variety of houses, Thetford is no exception. All sorts of buildings have provided dwelling space for Thetfordians, from large, stately mansions such as the King's House to the numerous, small, flint cottages. During the 1950s, one well known character about the town, Bill 'Patch-eye' Cook, even lived for a time in a Second World War pillbox on the edge of a field now occupied by Nunsgate.

The site of King's House was probably occupied by the medieval manor house of Thetford's manorial lords. Mr George W. Staniforth, the last resident of King's House, bequeathed the house to the town on his death in 1947. Since 1952 it has been the chambers and offices of Thetford Town Council. Part of King's House is now the Wayland District Registrar's office. The first marriage ceremony took place there in August 1993.

PAINTER'S STREET, c.1963

The most common type of dwelling to be found in 19th and early 20th century Thetford, was the terraced, flint cottage or house. Painter's Street [once Oldman's Lane] is a good example of working-class housing of this period. Painter's Street survived demolition when the 'inner-relief road' was built in 1967-68 but in 1973 it was decided that Painter's Street was to be demolished. Less than half of the original dwellings now survive. There were still about thirty dwellings in Painter's Street when this photograph was taken.

THE PRIORY, c.1920

Thetford is well known for its large number of medieval religious houses dissolved over four centuries ago. From the 12th to the 16th century this priory, dedicated to Saint Mary or Our Lady, was inhabited by a community of Cluniac monks. By the early years of the 20th century, however, the monks' former residence and what must have been a magnificent priory church, had become a well established ruin; numerous pieces of stone taken from Thetford's former religious houses can be seen built into the walls of several properties in the town. In the 1930s, after the site was placed in the care of the Ministry of Works, the ruins were properly excavated and preserved for posterity.

THETFORD WARREN LODGE, c.1915

The Warren Lodge, built in the 15th century as a fortified dwelling for warreners [also see page 17], stands on high ground about a mile from the western outskirts of the town but within what was the old Borough boundary. The Lodge was owned by the Duchy of Lancaster and was probably leased, along with the Great Warren, to the monks of Thetford's Cluniac priory.

At some time cottages were built on to the north and south sides of the lodge. Both cottages were occupied until the roof of the Warren Lodge and adjoining cottages were badly damaged by a fire in 1935. The cottages were then completely demolished leaving the ruins of the Lodge as they appear today, under the protection of English Heritage. It is said that a water well, one hundred feet deep, once supplied the inhabitants of this remote corner of the Borough.

THE CANONS' LODGE COTTAGES, c.1930

These small, thatched cottages stood on the Brandon Road, close to where the Canons' petrol station stood until very recently. They belonged to the Canons' Farm that once formed part of the Thetford Manor estate. In 1934, the estate was broken up into separate lots and sold. The Lodge Cottages, some of the last thatched buildings to survive in the town, were demolished in the mid-1960s just a few years before the old Canons' Barn, just visible in the background. [Photograph courtesy of the late Eric Pilbrow]

THE ANCIENT HOUSE, WHITE HART STREET, c.1905

On the left is the timber-framed Ancient House, one of Thetford's most cherished buildings. When originally built about the year 1490 it was a detached dwelling. Despite numerous alterations over the centuries, it still retains many fine features of Tudor architecture. When this photograph was taken, it was two separate dwellings but after it was purchased in 1921 by Prince Frederick Duleep Singh as a museum for the town, it was converted into something of its original form. After much renovation, the Ancient House Museum was opened by the Duchess of Grafton in December 1924.

Adjacent the Ancient House is the Kings Head public house, opposite is the first Thetford YMCA and further along the Working Men's Conservative Club, once a 19th century theatre.

CROXTON ROAD, c.1910

In the late 1890s and early 1900s, speculative builders and landowners built numerous detached, semi-detached and terraced houses, mostly on the outskirts of the town such as Croxton Road, Station Road, Norwich Road, Vicarage Road and Bury Road. These brick-built houses of a variety of designs and size, were a great improvement compared to the numerous, small, flint-built cottages in the town. These new town houses, although fairly modest in size, often displayed elaborate features found in the much larger houses of the very well-to-do.

CORPORATION DWELLINGS, c.1915

The Corporation Dwellings, built between 1912-14 just off the Bury Road, on a field that had previously been used as a playing field by the Boys' Grammar School, are Thetford's first municipal houses. They are also believed to be Norfolk's oldest surviving council houses. When completed, they helped to relieve the severe shortage of good quality housing for Thetford's 'working classes' at a cost of £6,675. Each house had a good sized garden, a feature omitted from many earlier working-class dwellings. The Dwellings were renamed as part of the St Mary's Estate in 1939 and finally named St Mary's Crescent in 1949. Locally they are more commonly called the 'White City'. In 1995 work began refurbishing and modernising, not for the first time, this land-mark in local housing.

NEWTOWN ESTATE, c.1922

Newtown's seventy-two houses were constructed in the early 1920s by local builder Sam Holden of Station Road. It was Thetford's second council estate and another step by the Corporation towards improving local housing needs and standards. The building of Newtown also fulfilled some of the promises made by the national government at the end of the Great War.

Despite new housing schemes, it was not until 1949-52 that the town had a modern sewage system. Moreover, nearly 400 of Thetford's 1,400 homes were still without electricity in 1950. [Photograph courtesy of the late Joyce Jones]

NEWTOWN ESTATE, c.1925

The Newtown Estate photographed soon after completion. In the distance is the tower of St Mary's Church and in the foreground the London Road. During the building of Newtown, large quantities of pottery known to be Late Saxon were discovered. The significance of this material lay unrecognised until further pottery found in early 1947 during the construction of Nelson Crescent was passed to T. C. Lethbridge, who then guessed that at least part of pre-Conquest Thetford must have been south of the rivers. This was confirmed by the excavations carried out between 1948-57 by Group Captain Guy Knocker.

THOMPSON'S ROW, c.1950

Thompson's Row [also erroneously known as Castle Row] stood just off Castle Street, behind Frank Clarke's ironmongers shop, where Rampart Way now links Castle Street with Raymond Street. It was named after George Thompson, a local timber merchant and cooper whose timber yard stood between Castle Street and Melford Common a century before this photograph was taken. Many of Thompson's employees once rented these dwellings from their employer. Although by the middle of the 20th century the tied-cottage or house was a rarity, many Thetfordians continued to rent their homes from a private landlord.

By the late 1950s Thompson's Row along with other similar properties in the town, with their outside privies and water taps, were classed as 'slum dwellings' and duly demolished. Thompson's Row was demolished in 1968 about two years after the last residents departed. [Photograph courtesy of Cecil Germany]

THE FULMERSTON ALMSHOUSES, BURY ROAD, 1968

The grim spectre of the workhouse was still very much a reality in the early years of the 20th century. However, not all paupers or aged poor people were confined to the Thetford Union Workhouse, many received assistance within the community, 'out-door relief' as it was called. A few aged poor were housed in one of Thetford's charity almshouses, maintained by the Trustees of the founder's charity. These almshouses were originally built for *'Two Old Men and Two Old Women'*, and were founded by the Will of Sir Richard Fulmerston who died in 1566/7. Sir Richard was interred in the nave of St Mary's Church, just across the road from where the almshouses stand.

In the late-1960s, John Howlett, a former Burrell apprentice, who left Thetford as a young man and became a wealthy businessman and Mayor of Lymington, Hampshire, paid for the refurbishment of the almshouses after they had become sadly neglected. In this photograph, painters put the finishing touches to the work. [Photograph courtesy of Thetford Town Council]

ST BARNABAS HOSPITAL, 1973 & ST BARNABAS CLOSE, 1995

Although it is generally the wealthiest who live in the largest houses, in the early years of the 20th century the poorest Thetfordians and those from the neighbouring parishes that once formed the Thetford Poor Law Union lived in what was the largest house for miles around.

The Workhouse, or 'Spike' as it was known, was built in 1836 to accommodate up to 300 paupers, although it never appears to have been 'home' or a refuge for more than about 200 inmates. The workhouse also provided some overnight shelter for the army of vagrants who were tramping the countryside well into the 1930s

The elected Boards of Guardians who administered the workhouse were officially abolished in 1929 and afterwards the old workhouse was utilised as an infirmary or hospital for the aged who were unable to have private care. It was then known as St Barnabas Hospital, the dedication of the little workhouse chapel built in the grounds of the workhouse in the 1860s.

St Barnabas Hospital closed in 1970. When this photograph was taken, the huge, red-brick, Victorian building was just about to be demolished. Twelve years later, a new residential estate known as St Barnabas Close was built on this infamous site, once a symbol of poverty and despair. [Photograph courtesy of Thetford Town Council]

QUEENSWAY, c.1955

These pre-fabricated council houses were built overlooking St Barnabas Hospital in 1953 and named Queensway to commemorate the new Queen, crowned that year. About the same time Hillary Road was built and named after Edmund Hillary the conqueror of Everest also in 1953.

13, SWEYN CLOSE, 1958

In the year following the Town Development Act 1952, it was suggested that Thetford might expand from a small, market town with an uncertain future to something more substantial. Thetford Borough Council made a formal approach to London County Council to be considered as a suitable London overspill town. After negotiations, it was agreed that Thetford would initially accommodate 5,000 Londoners. Plans were put forward and in 1957, an exhibition displaying Thetford's proposed Town Expansion was held in the Guildhall. The following year the building began.

In this photograph Mr Bill Jennings, Thetford Borough Surveyor, shows prospective settlers to the town some of the new houses under construction. Left-right: Bill Jennings, Mr & Mrs Ernie Farmer with their daughter Anita, Mr & Mrs B. Williams, Mr & Mrs Dennis Mead with their daughter Kay. [Photograph courtesy of Eastern Counties Newspapers]

FULMERSTON ROAD, c.1962

The first 'overspill' houses to be built and occupied were those in Sweyn Close and Fulmerston Road - linking the old with the new Thetford. It was at 58, Fulmerston Road in April 1959 that the Rural Dean of Thetford, the Reverend E. C. Brooks, conducted a special service to bless the *'overspill estate'*. By July 1959 the first 35 families had moved from London into their new Thetford homes. Fourteen months later, 107 houses had been completed, another 107 were under construction and tenders were being invited for a further 122 houses. The new Thetford had truly begun. [Photograph courtesy of Thetford Town Council]

ST MARTIN'S WAY, c.1965

The photographer was positioned almost directly above the Cemetery Lodge to capture this view of St Martin's Way, still under construction on the west-side of the London Road. St Martin's Way formed part of Red Castle Furze, the second large housing estate to be built in the 1960s. By 1970, nearly 2,000 new houses had been completed and work was well under way with the building of the Abbey Farm estate - a further 1,000 houses under the development scheme. [Photograph courtesy of Thetford Town Council]

PART OF THE BARNHAM CROSS ESTATE, 1974

In the foreground, children can be seen taking part in a sports event on the Elm Road School playing field. Elm Road runs horizontally across the view, houses spread beyond, westwards to the industrial estate, where the first new factories were built. Further to the west is the London Road and more factories. Also to be seen is the wooded Kimms Belt, a natural barrier between factories and houses. All this area was agricultural land until development began in the late 1950s. The Kimm family were millers and farmers in the middle of the 19th century. Their farm house and windmill stood beside the London Road, where the Norfolk Plover public house was built in 1966. [Photograph courtesy of the Ancient House Museum]

BURY ROAD ESTATES, 1974

After the completion of Newtown in the mid-1920s, Thetford Borough Council built no more homes until 1938 when work began on the St Mary's Estate, just off the Bury Road. The Corporation Dwellings, built before the Great War, were added to the estate in 1939. In 1948 the estate comprised a total of 112 houses.

Work began building more council houses almost immediately after the 1939-45 War. Nelson Crescent, Fulmerston Road, Icknield Way, Saxon Place and Williamson Crescent were created to accommodate some of the 180 families then waiting to be housed. The houses that formed the St Mary's Estate were named Nelson Crescent, St Margaret's Crescent and St Mary's Crescent.

In the same part of the town during the 1950s, other new roads were built and lined with houses, Fulmerston Close, Hillary Road, Icknield Close, Staniforth Road and Queensway. New housing extended along Fulmerston Road and the Bury Road.

Easily recognisable in this view, taken from the south, is the Gas Works on the Bury Road - the Bury Road runs diagonally across the picture. To the west of the Bury Road are the council estates built between 1912-1955. East of the Bury Road and south of the Gas Works can be seen St Michael's Close and St Edmund's Court, built in the early 1970s. Further to the east is Nunsgate, a private development started in 1964. It is interesting to note that buried beneath many of these houses are the archaeological remains of Thetford's pre-Conquest houses.

On the northern horizon is the Abbey Farm estate, one of the last GLC housing developments in the town. Work on the Abbey Farm estate began in 1967 and the first families settled there in 1970.

In 1996, work began on constructing Water Mill Green, a private residential development, on land once occupied by the Pulp Mill between Mill Lane and the Bury Road. [Photograph courtesy of the Ancient House Museum]

ST GILES' LANE, 1970

Large numbers of houses in old parts of the town, such as St Giles' lane, Pike Lane and St Nicholas Street, were demolished in the 1960s and 70s as part of the Town Development.

These houses stand empty, waiting demolition to make way for a car park and service road to the rear of King Street. The building in the left foreground has survived, however, and is now Boot's opticians department.
[Photograph courtesy of Rita Christian]

ST NICHOLAS STREET, c.1965

St Nicholas Street is now unrecognisable from that of just thirty years ago, even though an old maltings, a scrap yard and a few houses at the north end still survive. Changes began to take place in St Nicholas Street with the demolition of a few poor-quality cottages in the early 1960s. A more radical upheaval took place when the 'inner-relief road' was constructed in 1968 bisecting the street; the road passes through just about where the pedestrian can be seen in the photograph.

The houses and Co-op store that stand in the distance on the left or east side of the street were demolished in the early 1970s. This site became a car park until 1990 when it was excavated by archaeologists prior to construction of new offices for Breckland District Council. [Photograph courtesy of Thetford Town Council]

EARLS STREET, c.1905

Not all of Thetford's town centre streets have drastically changed their appearance since the early years of the 20th century. Parts of Earls Street, Castle Street and Magdalen Street would easily be recognised by past generations. What is noticeable in this particular photograph compared with Earls Street today, is the difference in the surface of the road and the absence of motor cars.

BRANDON ROAD, 1995

Smoke rises from beneath a pot of food, cooking above an open fire. These modern-day Romany gypsies are camped on what was the car park of the former Warrener public house. Gypsies and travellers have been passing through the town for centuries, sometimes stopping off on one of the local commons or open spaces for a few days before travelling on to some other destination. The arrival and presence of gypsies has often provoked hostility from nearby house dwellers.

The gaily painted, wooden, horse-drawn gypsy vans seen earlier in the century, have generally been replaced by modern caravans, invariably towed by a motor vehicle. It would appear, from the numbers of touring caravans owned by house dwellers in the town, that many more of us crave for a life-style of travelling with our home in tow, if only for a few weeks in the summer months.

Undoubtedly Thetford's best remembered caravan dweller is chimney sweep, Jimmy Nicholls [1870-1953], who lived and traded for many years from an old wooden van parked on a small plot of land in St Mary's Row, beside St Mary's churchyard.

SPEEDWELL CLOSE, CLOVERFIELDS, 1995

Since the 'boom' house building years between the late 1950s and 1980, when hundreds of council and private residential properties were built in the town, there has been a more modest growth. This is also reflected in Thetford's population statistics [see page 5]. The Cloverfields Estate, built across the ancient Green Lane on land between the river Thet and the Norwich Road, is the largest recent development in the town since building began in the early 1980s. In 1984 four-bedroom houses on the new estate were being advertised for £39,995. Four years later a local newspaper reported, *'Thetford has virtually run out of any house in any street, for less than £40,000'*. Within a few months of this report, houses prices began to fall rapidly, leaving many with so-called negative equity.

An important feature of the modern house is the garage, sometimes an integral part of the building. Gardens are now more likely to be landscaped with flowers and shrubs, rather than vegetables and fruit. Poultry and livestock, once commonly kept in the garden are now a rarity. Moreover, very few householders now maintain an allotment for growing produce.

SAXON PLACE, 1995

The last two of the twenty pre-fabricated Airey houses built by Thetford Borough Council 1950-51 wait demolition. These are Thetford's first council-built houses to be demolished. Undoubtedly in future years, like Saxon Place, others will follow to be replaced by more modern buildings. When John & Audrey Osborne moved into number 10 in 1951, their weekly rent was 19s 7d [98p] and John's wage as a labourer about £4 15s [£4.75]. When they finally moved out in 1995, their rent had increased to over £40 a week while receiving a joint State Pension of £106.

After Thetford Borough Council's demise in 1974, as a result of local government reorganisation, Thetford's large, council housing stock came under the control of the newly created Breckland District Council. New legislation placed this responsibility in the hands of Peddars Way Housing Association in 1993.

THE NORTHERN RESIDENTIAL ESTATES, 1995

The photographer, positioned high above Rosemary Musker High School [bottom left corner] and Ann Bartholomew Road just off the Croxton Road, captures an interesting view of the residential estates constructed north of the old town centre since the late 1950s. The first of these developments can be seen in the top-right corner: Norfolk Road and the Redgate private estate. Redgate was a working farm until sold for development in 1957 and in 1959 work began extending the north end of Magdalen Street by building old people's bungalows and creating Norfolk Road.

The Cloverfields development which began in 1983 and is still in progress [also see page 101], can be seen to the left or north of Redgate, divided from Redgate by Hurth Way that follows the route of the former Thetford - Bury railway line [also see page 48]. Work began developing the open fields between the Norwich Road and the main railway in the mid-1960s. On the opposite side of the railway, on the wedge of land towards the Croxton Road, building began in the late 1960s: Highlands in 1967 and Fairfields in 1970. [Photograph by Derek A. Edwards (courtesy of Norfolk Museum Services), 19 June 1995. Ref: TL8784/[illegible]/HBV16]

AT REST & PLAY

'Holiday time is upon us once more, and I hope that you will all have an opportunity to get away and have a rest and a change. We should not forget how fortunate we are in these days to be able to have our holidays in this way - it has not always been so'.

The Reverend Peter Moore, 'Saint Mary-the-Less, Thetford; Parish Magazine', August 1965

EX-SERVICEMEN'S BOWLS CLUB, c.1935

Thetfordians have pursued all sorts of games, sports and activities for recreation and pleasure. Some of these leisure pursuits have ancient origins while others are relatively new. Moreover, some pursuits have lasted the test of time, while others have not. Bowls has been played out-doors in the summer months for centuries. Although there are only two bowling greens in the town today compared with about six in the first quarter of the century, its popularity as a game has not really dwindled.

This photograph of the Ex-Service Bowls Club [which is still in existence today], includes Mr George W. Staniforth [seated three from the left in the front row] of the King's House, a very keen bowls player. The Staniforth Bowls Club now play in the garden of the King's House, Mr Staniforth's former home. The Staniforth Club traditionally marked the beginning of each season with a match against Thetford Borough Council.

THETFORD CRICKET CLUB, 1905

Compared with bowls, cricket is a new sport. However, Thetford's cricketing tradition reaches back at least to 1806 when a Thetford team played Gooderstone and Hilborough on Lynford Plains. Earlier this century, when this photograph was taken, cricket continued to be one of those sports that removed age-old class barriers, as local gentry could be found playing alongside labourers.

Back row, left-right: A. Sayer, F. Haysman, E. Claydon, L.D. Stilman, R. Barber, W. Wagg, F. Carter, E. C. Turner, H. Jessop, G. Blaydon [captain]. Front row: R. Randall, W. Sparrow, H. Campkin.

One of Thetford's greatest moments in local cicketing history took place in 1975 when Thetford CC won the prestigious Carter Cup by beating Mundford CC at Lakenham in an exciting final.

THETFORD TOWN FOOTBALL CLUB, 1909

At the beginning of the century, Association Football had been played in Thetford for about twenty-five years. This photograph was taken at the Recreation Ground just four years after the new pavilion was opened. Until then, Thetford's cricketers and footballers had little choice but to change their clothing under the shelter of a nearby hedge. Perhaps this Thetford team had benefited from the visit in 1907 of Mr J. W. Bowman, manager of Norwich City F.C., who gave a lecture in the Guildhall, *'Football and How To Play It'*.

Back row, left-right: G. R. Blaydon [Hon. Gen. and Fin. Secretary], F. J. Barwood, W. Sparrow, A. Davis, J.G. Brown [Chairman]. Centre row: W. E. Wagg, A. Foulger, E. Claydon [Capt], R.M. Palmer, W. Clarke, F. Crick. Front row: W. Ruddock, W. Woods. [R. M. Palmer played for Norwich City F.C., between 1902-04.]

THETFORD TOWN F.C. - WINNERS OF THE NORFOLK SENIOR CUP, 1948

Thousands of Thetfordians travelled by road and rail to Carrow Road, Norwich, in March 1948 to support Thetford Town who were playing in the final of the Norfolk Senior Cup for the first time in their history. The final against North Walsham ended in a 2-2 draw, C. Flack and J. Middleton scoring for Thetford. In the replay the following week, Thetford were victorious winning 4 - 2 with goals from L. James, D. Grey, H. Eggleton [2].

Back row, left-right: J. Bullen, A. Mayes, P. James, H. Rix, K. Makins, H. Jordan. Front row: H. Eggleton, L. James, D. Grey, J. Middleton, G. Barnes. [Photograph courtesy of Percy James]

THETFORD ROVERS FOOTBALL CLUB, 1952

Besides the Town club, there was also a Thetford Rovers F.C. in the very early years of the century. The Rovers played on one of Mr Musker's fields near the Melford Bridge but appear to have disbanded by 1905. A new Thetford Rovers F.C. was formed and in their first season played in the South Norfolk League 1951-52. Founder members included George Angus, snr, Pat Fayers, 'Curly' Robinson and Ted Zipfel. In the early 1950s, home matches were played on one of Mr Kent's fields just off the London Road, close to where the Norfolk Plover public house stood from 1966 until demolished in 1996.

Back row, left-right: Alan Mayes, John Waldron, Brian Backshall, Dennis Wharf, Hopkinson, Peter Bidwell, 'Jessie' Hall, George Angus. Front row: Bertie Lockwood, Edward 'Ted' Zipfel, Geoff MacDonald, John Fayers, Alan Harrington.

THETFORD RUGBY CLUB, 1960

Thetford Rugby Club was officially formed in January 1960 by a group of local business men. That same month they won their first game, beating the Norfolk School of Agriculture at Kilverstone Park, their new home ground. Two years later, the club moved to RAF Honington for eight years, then RAF Barnham and in 1972 to their present ground at Two Mile Bottom where the club runs eight senior and junior teams and a veterans' side. This photograph is of the original founder members and players at Kilverstone.

The players: back row, left-right: Alec 'Sandy' Witton, -?-, Mike Robinson, -?-, Des Allen, Andy Dolling, -?-, Rob Hook. Centre row, left-right: Charles Watson, Ron Baroll, David Cunningham, Dennis Carnelly, -?-, Peter Penny, David Christopher, Ian Clarke. Front row: -?-, -?-, -?-, J. Smith. Others include Neville Bishop, Frank Kemp, George Kybird, Captain Jones, Bill Jennings, Tom Jessup, John Clark, Peter Cook and Evan Harris. [Photograph courtesy of Thetford Rugby Club]

THETFORD GOLF CLUB, c. 1914

Thetford Golf Club was formed and the golf course laid-out in 1912, many years after the game of golf was first established. Thetford's 18 hole course, or links as it was often called, was built west of the town on part of the Great Warren, ancient heathland and once a natural habitat for thousands of rabbits.

After a northern bypass route was decided in 1987 part of the original golf course had to be abandoned. A new course was designed and constructed to allow for the new road. The old club house seen in this view was converted into a veterinary surgery in 1980, after a new golf club house was built further to the west and south of the Brandon Road.

When this photograph was taken, golf was still very much a recreation for the wealthier sections of Thetford society, and those unable to afford membership fees could earn a few shillings by acting as caddies.

MR SAM PARRISH, 1912

Thetford's rivers continue to provide sport for anglers of all ages, as they did when Sam Parrish landed this catch of over 14 pounds in August 1912.

Besides fishing, the rivers are an ideal setting and venue for a variety of other water activities. Canoes and other small, water-craft can sometimes be seen navigating the narrow waterways. Children can be found paddling in the shallows or feeding the numerous ducks and swans that have made Thetford their habitat. Picturesque walks have been created along the river banks and there is much to interest artists, photographers and naturalists.

THE COUNCIL SWIMMING BATHS, c.1925

The Council Swimming Baths, situated on the Little Ouse river near the Nun's Bridges, were once a favourite resort for Thetfordians during the summer months, particularly if the weather was hot. Hundreds of children and adults could be seen enjoying the water or sunbathing on the grass bank opposite.

Wooden bathing sheds were first erected here in the 1890s, and in the early 1920s a concrete bank and other improvements were made. The Council Baths became redundant after the opening of an indoor pool on the Croxton Road in 1972.

THETFORD DOLPHINS SWIMMING CLUB, 1988 & 89

Thetford Dolphins Amateur Swimming Club was formed in 1971 by the late Tony Hegarty. Now affiliated to the Amateur Swimming Association, the club competes in league and trophy galas, including visits to Holland and Germany against teams from Thetford's twin towns.

The top photograph was taken at the Club Championships in 1988. Mr Ben Culey, the Club President, can be seen with junior club members: Mark Ewing, James Barrett and Gerry Harris. The photograph below was taken at a club training session at the Croxton Road pool in 1989, five years before it was destroyed by fire. Work began constructing a new pool on the site in 1995. [Photograph courtesy of Thetford Dolphins ASC]

ST MARY'S CHURCH, c.1910 & 1996

At the beginning of the century, the Church played an important part in many more people's lives. And even if people did not attend one of the three ancient parish churches or one of the many non-conformist chapels in the town, Sunday remained a special day, a day of rest. The nearest thing to any form of entertainment on a Sunday was the sound of church bands, bells and music. Children were discouraged from playing in the street and there were few public activities in which to participate. Even the local cinema and swimming baths were kept closed on Sundays into the middle of this century and drinking hours were restricted.

Throughout much of this century, as in the past, the fabric of St Mary's Church has been altered and repaired. One of the most noticeable changes was the removal of the belfry, lowering the tower by over twenty feet in 1968. Two years later, despite an increasing number of people living in this part of the town, St Mary's Church was last regularly used for public worship by the local Anglican community. From 1981 until 1986, however, it was taken over as an additional place of worship, by Thetford's Roman Catholic Church. Since then, St Mary's has been redundant. It now stands sadly neglected, many of its former interior furnishings vandalised or removed, while awaiting a new owner and an alternative use after centuries of religious devotion by past parishioners.

THETFORD SALVATION ARMY BAND, c.1910

Music has been described as *'the food of life'* and it has certainly figured prominently in the leisure activities of many Thetfordians. Live music was the only source of musical entertainment in the early years of the century but the appearance of the gramophone and the wireless provided popular alternatives.

In the centre of this photograph, holding the baton, is bandmaster George A. Reeve, believed to have been the first permanent bandmaster when the Thetford Corps was formed in 1887. Seated on his left is his son, Edwin Reeve, bandmaster from 1921-1952 who in turn was succeeded by his son, Wesley.

Throughout most of the century Thetford's Salvation Army Band has been seen and heard touring the town on Sunday mornings and on other occasions, playing an assortment of stirring hymns and marches.

HECTOR SUTHERLAND'S NEW RHYTHM BAND, c.1930

All sorts of musical events have been performed and enjoyed by 20th century Thetfordians. The 1920s and 30s saw the rise in popularity of the dance band. Perhaps Thetford's most famous dance band was that formed by Hector Sutherland in 1928. Hector had played as a professional musician in London and Europe with some of the best dance and jazz musicians around before settling in Thetford and forming his own band. The popularity of the New Rhythm Band soon spread; their music could be heard at dance and concert halls across East Anglia until the out-break of war in 1939.

Left-right: -?-, banjo; Ernest 'Bunny' Bowes, drums; George Challice, saxophone; Bill Wright, bass; Hector Sutherland, saxophone; Marjorie Sutherland, piano; Harold Bowes, trumpet. [Photograph courtesy of Peter Bowes]

THE RED BOWES BAND, c.1950

The Red Bowes Band was formed about 1947, evolving from an earlier band - the St John's Jive Cadets - a group of young people who were members of the St John Ambulance Brigade and interested in jazz music. The St John's Jive Cadets first public engagement was at the VE Celebration Dances held at the Guildhall in May 1945. After Harold Bowes and Florence Greenough joined the original band members in 1947, the Red Bowes Band continued in the music traditions set by Hector Sutherland's band, and played at many local dances and concerts, including Paul Greenough's immensely popular 'Rock and Roll Show' at the Oddfellows' Hall in the early 1950s. This photograph was taken at a dance in the Old Maltings, Old Market Street.

Left-right: Peter Dennis, bass; George Warren, clarinet; Peter 'Red' Bowes, drums; Harold Bowes, trumpet; Florence Greenough piano. Other musicians who also played with the band at different times include 'Bunny' Bowes, 'Dickie' Bird, Osborne Ladell and Evelyn Young. [Photograph courtesy of Peter Bowes]

OLD TIME DANCE CLUB, c.1950

After the war Thetford's Old Time Dancing Club held regular dances in the Breckland Hall, the former Oddfellows' Hall in Earls Street. At these popular dances, the Red Bowes Band played as a trio: Harold Bowes, violin, Peter 'Red' Bowes, drums and Mrs Florence Greenough, piano. [Photograph courtesy of Peter Bowes]

THE FIVE-SIDED SQUARES, c.1957

In the mid-to-late 1950s, Thetford's teenagers were caught up in both the skiffle and rock-and-roll craze that swept through the country, helped by the increasing popularity of television and 45 rpm vinyl record discs. The Five-Sided Squares, hoping to emulate the success of the acclaimed kings of skiffle, Lonnie Donegan and Bob Cort and the Vipers, are seen rehearsing in St Mary's Church Hall.

The Five-Sided Squares changed their name, line-up and musical style several times before finally disbanding as a rock-and-roll band in 1962. Left-right: Mike Burton, guitar; Ken Wright, tea-chest bass; David Allison, vocals; Robin Fuller, wash-board and drums; Pat Pearson, guitar. [Photograph courtesy of Michael Burton]

THE THETFORD SINGERS, 1992

Although there have always been a number of capable choirs singing in local churches and chapels and a Thetford Operatic Society in the early years of the century, Thetford was not especially renowned for its choral singing before the Thetford Singers were established in 1974.

From about fifteen choristers, the Singers now number about sixty, drawn from a wide area of Norfolk and Suffolk. The Thetford Singers perform up to six concerts each year in Thetford and the surrounding district, attracting lovers of classical choral music. Many of these concerts, performed in ancient churches, are accompanied by an orchestra or ensemble of local semi-professional musicians. This photograph was taken at a concert held in Thetford's Carnegie Room. [Photograph courtesy of Barry Griggs]

THE PALACE CINEMA, 1983

It seems likely that, at some time in the early 1900s, the first screening of silent movies or the 'flicks' in Thetford took place in a travelling showman's tent on the Market Place. The Oddfellows' Hall was first used as an impromptu cinema, and in 1913 Thetford's first purpose-built cinema, known as the Electric Cinema, was built and opened on this site in Guildhall Street. 'Talkies' were shown here for the first time in 1931 and it was probably during the next two decades, before television made its impact, that the Palace Cinema enjoyed its most popular days. At that time Sunday cinema shows were prohibited and it was not until the late 1940s before this restriction was lifted, even then, a percentage of the Sunday takings had to be paid to local charities.

Despite the increasing number of televisions in the home [BBC was obtainable in Thetford from 1953 and ITV from 1959] the Palace Cinema survived until 1984. Since then it has been completely refurbished as a venue for the popular game of bingo, offering the chance of substantial money prizes.

PALACE THETFORD 'Phone 2279

Sunday, May 25th, 6 and 8.30 p.m.—
Alan Ladd in **The Glass Key** and **Tokyo Rose**

Mon., May 26th, and Tues. 6 and 8.30 p.m. Wed 7 p.m.
MICHAEL REDGRAVE, JEAN KENT in

The Browning Version

Also **CACTUS CARAVAN**

Thurs., May 29th, Fri. and Sat. 6 and 8.30 p.m. Mats. Thurs. 2.30, Sat. 2 p.m.
Filmed in Technicolor with
TONY CURTIS, PIPER LAURIE

The Prince who was a Thief

Also **DEATH IN THE HAND**

MINSTERGATE, 1994

For a few months in 1994, a cinema reappeared in the town with the opening in Minstergate of Diamond Screens, a new cinema with two studios. A lack of patronage, however, soon brought about its closure.

KING STREET, 1950

The fashionable and popular Anglian Café and Milk Bar was opened in 1950 by Mr Ben Culey, the proprietor of the Palace Cinema. The following year, during the Festival of Britain week, the Palm Beach Quartet from London played there each evening.

The Festival of Britain was a celebration of Britain's achievements in science, industry and the arts. Thetford's Festival week was opened on the 4th June 1951 by the Lord Lieutenant of Norfolk, Sir Edmund Bacon. Thetford's activities included a model steam engine exhibition, an exhibition of 18th century life, a Thomas Paine exhibition, a shop window-dressing competition for the town's traders, national dancing, music concerts and a parade of decorated vehicles on the Market Place, watched by a reported crowd of 4,000 people.

The premises once occupied by the Anglian Café are now Stead & Simpson's shoe shop.

BURY ROAD, c.1960

The Thetford Lodge of Royal Antediluvian Order of Buffaloes [RAOB] wearing their regalia, parade along the Bury Road towards St Mary's Church for their special annual church service.

Organisations such as the Buffs, as they are commonly known, have been holding their meetings in the town for many years. Like the local friendly societies of Oddfellows and Foresters, who were particularly active in the town during the 19th and first half of the 20th century, the RAOB fosters a sense of mutual fellowship and welfare amongst its membership. Thetford Priory Lodge RAOB now have their headquarters on the Bury Road, moving there from the Station Road. [Photograph courtesy of Bill Leeder]

BURY ROAD, c.1975

Members of Thetford's Labour Club are about to embark on a day-trip by motor coach to Great Yarmouth. Coach outings to the sea-side have been a popular event on the itinerary of local clubs and societies for many years. Included in the above photograph is Matt Elliot, Paddy and Mrs Smart, Mrs Pratt, Dolly James, Eva Nimmo, Rene Cook, George Richardson, May Leeder, Jack Hunter, May Page, Mrs Lockwood, Jack King, Ted Flint, Mr Dow, Bill Lockwood and Grace Page. [Photograph courtesy of May Leeder]

WHIT-MONDAY FETE, 1967

Until the 1990s local fêtes and carnivals have always featured in the local calendar, usually attracting a good crowd. An estimated 5,000 are reported to have attended this annual Whit-Monday fête organised by Thetford Rotary Club and Thetford Round Table and held on the Recreation Ground. Amongst the many attractions to amuse the crowds were bowling for a pig, a donkey 'Derby' and this roller horse. [Photograph courtesy of Eastern Counties Newspapers]

MAY DAY CARNIVAL, 1985

Hundreds of people line the river bank and the Town Bridge to view a raft race contested on the Little Ouse river. The carnival was one of many organised by Thetford (Breckland) Lions to raise money for charities.

Other popular attractions on this occasion included numerous charity stalls lining King Street and the Riverside Walk. Crowds thronged the stalls, buying all sorts of goods - much of it second-hand and donated for charity - or attempted to win a lucky prize.

MARKET PLACE, 1988

Thetford's May Day carnival in 1988 included amusement rides on the Market Place. This was probably the first time that fairground rides had been seen on the Market Place since the 1920s and 30s when steam engines were still being used to power the attractions and generate electricity to illuminate the fair.

Several other places in the town have been used, at different times during the century, as a fairstead. They include a field just off the Station Road, land on the west side of the Bury Road where a petrol station stands today, and the Melford Common where amusement fairs are still held.

AUGUST BANK HOLIDAY CARNIVAL, 1994

Crowds gather around the School Lane car park and Coffee Mill. They are enjoying the atmosphere of a carnival organised to raise funds for local charities and organisations. Amongst the attractions was 'live' music from a pop band, fire appliances from the local fire station and lots of side-shows, including a contest of strength by pulling a motor lorry.

THETFORD FESTIVAL, 1996

In June, the Mayor, Pat Pearson, opened the Thetford Festival from the steps of the Guildhall. The Festival was organised to put Thetford 'on the map' and to increase awareness and appreciation of the arts in the town and surrounding district. This was the first Thetford Festival since June 1958 when a religious play, telling the story of the Creation until the Last Judgement, was performed in the Castle Park.

The opening programme of the 1996 Festival included a performance on the Market Place by the Abbey Twirlettes, seen in this photograph, and Beating the Retreat by the Norwich Pipe Band. An International Day followed and there were other dancing, drama and music activities during the week, culminating in a concert held in the Priory ruins, performed by the newly formed Thetford Concert Orchestra and the Norfolk Symphony Orchestra in front of several hundred people. Amongst the exhibitions held during the Festival Week was 'Thetford – A Century Remembered' in the Ancient House Museum.

TOWN CENTRE CHANGES

'The whole thing has taken a while to integrate. On balance it has certainly been for the better. It has its problems. You can't introduce a substantially imported population into an area without upsetting some of the natives'.
Local businessman, Mr Paul Rackham, discussing Thetford's development. From an interview published in the Eastern Daily Press Business Supplement, 10 April 1991

THETFORD TOWN CENTRE 1932

Change is nothing new to the appearance of Thetford. Throughout its history, even before the word 'overspill' had any meaning locally, there have been numerous small-scale changes and developments to many parts of the town but particularly the town centre - the streets that radiate from the Guildhall and Market Place. These changes may have been the modernisation of old buildings, simply by the construction of a new and fashionable facade, or the complete demolition of a building or block of buildings, to make way for new, modern structures. Moreover, at times, gardens and orchards have gradually disappeared, very often, by 'piecemeal' developments.

This view taken in the early 1930s, looking along Raymond Street and Guildhall Street, remained virtually unaltered until the early 1960s when, within two decades, the landscape changed enormously with the demolition of many old buildings and the construction of new. However, although much that can be seen in this fascinating photograph has been swept away by progress, the basic street pattern remains virtually unchanged and the Guildhall and Market Place easily recognisable landmarks. Note the haphazard assortment of buildings that infill the land behind the street fronts. [Photograph courtesy of Aerofilms Limited]

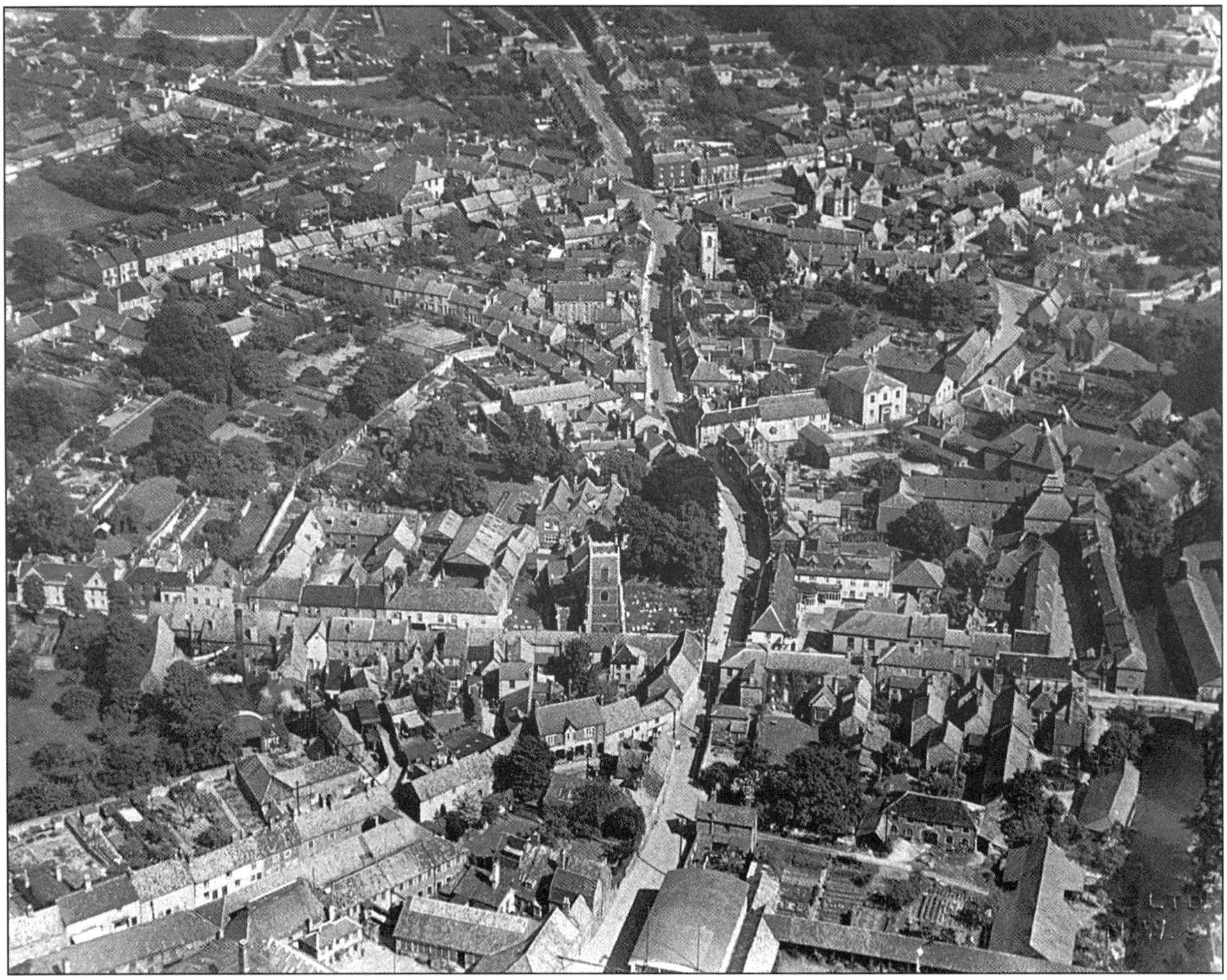

THETFORD VIEWED FROM THE WEST, 1932

This view looks eastwards, along the line of Minstergate, King Street and Castle Street, a road feature that has probably been part of Thetford's topography for at least 800 years. Although, as in the previous photograph, it is a vastly different scene today, many important structures have survived to form a part of Thetford's ancient heritage. In the foreground is the former Burrell paint shop, now the Charles Burrell Museum. To the right, the cast-iron Town Bridge spans the Little Ouse river. St Peter's Church stands opposite the Bell Hotel and the King's House and St Cuthbert's Church are easily recognisable today.

The year before this photograph was taken, Thetford's population was officially recorded at 4,135. In 1959, when Thetford began to expand as an 'overspill' town, the population had increased to about 4,700. [Photograph courtesy of Aerofilms Limited]

THE GUILDHALL, c.1899

The first significant structural change to take place in the town centre at the beginning of the 20th century was the construction of a new Guildhall, replacing this one that had been built exactly a century earlier.

THE GUILDHALL AND MARKET PLACE, c.1959

When officially opened in 1902, the new Guildhall was described as *'a splendid public building, which forms a striking and handsome feature in the town'*. Besides providing a common hall for all sorts of activities, the Guildhall was the chambers and offices for Thetford Borough Council until 1952.

To the right of the Guildhall is the 19th century covered market accommodation known as the Shambles, converted into shop units in 1986. Although the Guildhall remains almost unaltered, the Market Place has been refurbished several times since the early years of the century.

OPENING OF THE SALVATION ARMY CITADEL, 1910

Another new building erected in the early years of the 20th century was the Salvation Army Citadel in Magdalen Street. It was another welcomed improvement to the appearance of the town. Less than two years later a new YMCA was built next-door. Both buildings were erected through the generosity of Josiah Vavasseur [1834 - 1908] of Kilverstone Hall.

RUINS OF THE FRIENDS' MEETING HOUSE, CAGE LANE, c.1905

Thetford's Quakers built a meeting house under the shadow of the Guildhall in 1696. Once thatched, it was already ruinous when this photograph was taken and had completely disappeared by the mid-1920s, if not before.

The site of the Meeting House is now covered by the forecourt of the Carnegie Room which opened in 1968. Before construction work began on the Carnegie Room, a number of interments in the small, Quakers' burial ground were removed to the London Road cemetery.

THE TOWN CAGE, 1963

The Town Cage or Lock-up stood beside the Friends' Meeting House. It was demolished in 1966 to make way for the Guildhall extension - the Carnegie Room. The Town Stocks, once held in the Town Cage, are now housed in a new building opposite the Carnegie Room.

GUILDHALL STREET, c.1910

This view looks towards the Market Place, the old Post Office can be seen in the distance. On the left foreground is the main store of the Thetford Co-operative Society. The Co-op gradually extended its premises along the west side of the street before being completely demolished in 1989.

The sign-board of the Dog and Partridge public house can be seen. The Dog closed its doors in 1971 and was demolished soon afterwards to make way for new shops. Another building that disappeared just a few years earlier was the former Primitive Methodist Chapel, that stood on the corner with Cage Lane.

GUILDHALL STREET, 1965

The former Primitive Methodist Chapel, built in the 1860s, has almost disappeared. As soon as the site was cleared, work begun constructing the so-called Red Cross building, opened in January 1967. [Photograph courtesy of Thetford Town Council]

INTERIOR OF PRIMITIVE METHODIST CHAPEL, c.1910

After the union of the Methodist Churches in the early 1930s, the chapel was no longer used for regular religious worship. It later became a public hall, known as the Central Hall.

GUILDHALL STREET, 1995

From a street of some charm and character - a mixture of commercial and residential buildings - just four decades ago, Guildhall Street now presents an unappealing landscape - a confusion of different architectural styles, both old and new. Perhaps saddest of all are the vacant building plots that have become overgrown with vegetation in the long wait for redevelopment. [Photograph courtesy of Carl Richards]

WELL STREET, c.1925

Well Street's attractive mixture of cottages and houses remained very much unchanged until demolition began on the east side of the street for the Guildhall extension - the Carnegie Room - in 1965. At the far end of Well Street, on the corner of Tanner Street, stood the Melbourne Hotel, opened as a Temperance Hotel in the last quarter of the last century. The building that appears to stand across the end of the street is the ancient Manor House.

THE MANOR HOUSE, 1967

When this photograph was taken, the Manor House was already being demolished to make way for the Thetford County Library. Thetford Borough Council's decision to demolish the Manor House was taken after an architectural survey and a great amount of debate. However, when the final decision had to be made the Mayor, Councillor James T. Waters' vote decided the issue by six votes to five.

In the 1920s, marriage ceremonies took place at the Manor House, then 2, Raymond Street, the Superintendent Registrar's Office. Little else is known of the history of the Manor House but from its name and appearance, it ought to have been a long and interesting one. [Photograph courtesy of Thetford Town Council]

WELL STREET, 1968

By April 1968, as the last of Well Street's old buildings quickly fall into heaps of rubble, the Manor House is no more than a memory. In the right foreground is Allison's shop from where sweets, chocolates and tobacco were sold until the previous year. [Photograph courtesy of Rita Christian]

WELL STREET, 1995

Well Street was transformed into this row of shops with flats above in the late-1960s. Perhaps, when we look at what has replaced those charming and attractive buildings that once stood there, we may wonder how Thetford Borough Council could have taken such decisions.

The County Library, standing at the far end of the street on the site of the old Manor House, was opened in 1970. From 1952 until the opening of the new library, the old Mechanics' Institute on the Market Place served as the County Library. It then became a doctor's surgery, afterwards a wine bar known as the Tipsy Toad and then another wine bar named the Old Library. [Photograph courtesy of Carl Richards]

KING STREET, c.1925

How many can remember King Street as it appears in this photograph? Most of the buildings on the right were replaced by new shops with flats above in the early 1960s. It is a scene without people or vehicles, apart from a Savage Bros hand-cart standing in front of the ancient edifice of St Cuthbert's Church. In 1971, the surrounding churchyard was paved without disturbing any burials and surviving headstones were placed as a feature in the surrounding walls. That same year Anglican services became centred on St Cuthberts.

KING STREET, 1955

King Street changed little in the first half of the 20th century. The road surface and pavements improved and new shop-fronts and shopkeepers appeared but otherwise the street was as easily recognisable as that at the beginning of the century.

As people gaze into Savage's shop window, little could they have known that this familiar scene was soon to change drastically. Less than a decade later, Savage Bros and other old established shops that lined each side of King Street disappeared. More were soon to follow, to be replaced by new shop premises and shopkeepers.

King Street had been made 'One Way' to traffic in 1957 but another significant change took place in 1974 when King Street was closed to vehicular traffic and work began on pedestrianising Thetford's principle high street. [Photograph courtesy of Studio Five, Thetford]

KING STREET, c.1925

On the left is Robert Rinder's dairy. Opposite is the King's Arms Inn, closed in 1927 and demolished in the mid-1930s to make way for new shops - one of the few town centre developments to take place in the 1930s. Another was the building of a new Post Office in 1939.

KING STREET, c.1938

On the left is Rinder's old dairy, then occupied by Scott's drapery shop. Opposite stands the new showrooms of the British Gas Light and Coke Company and a branch shop of Savage Bros on the site of the old King's Arms Inn. It was in King Street that the first town centre changes of the early 1960s began. Brown's hardware store and a large, old house that stood next door that served as a nursing home for a few years, were demolished to make way for Woolworth's store opened in 1961.

The nursing home made national news in 1937, when a Mrs Lingwood of Brandon gave birth to quads there. The gas showrooms closed in 1994.

Telephone: 3239

ADDERLEY'S

High-Class Bakers & Confectioners

WEDDING & BIRTHDAY
CAKES A SPECIALITY

7 KING STREET - THETFORD
NORFOLK

KING STREET, 1995

Shoppers walk through the traffic-free King Street on a fine mid-week morning in February. Despite the many changes brought about by new shop premises and pedestrianisation, it is not too difficult to visualise the street as it was. At least today one can stand in the middle of the street and 'mardle' without the fear of being run over by motor traffic.

In January 1996 work began reshaping and improving the general appearance of King Street by laying new paving stones and erecting new street furniture. [Photograph courtesy of Carl Richards]

KING STREET, c.1938

Another view that has changed dramatically since the mid-1960s, although some buildings have survived. The row of shops on the right, standing between the King's House and the entrance to St Giles Lane, have retained very little of their original structure. Since the early 1960s they have either been completely rebuilt or given a new facade, generally sympathetic and in keeping with the original architecture.

Opposite is the Tanner Street junction and in the left foreground, Robert Pett's old house, demolished in the mid-1960s along with the house on the opposite corner of Tanner Street, once the home of Dr Minns.

Further along the street can be seen J.W. Clarke's stationery and newsagents shop, now T & W Wines. It was outside Clarke's shop in 1953 that Thetford's first permanent electric street light was erected.

TANNER STREET, 1960

Besides the major changes that took place, often involving the demolition of old buildings and the construction of new, many buildings have also been renovated, sometimes for a completely different use. This old furniture warehouse, owned by Glasswell's of Bury St Edmunds, was purchased by Thetford's Methodists in 1960 and opened the following year as a Church Hall, an extension of the existing 19th century chapel. Early in the 19th century all this land formed part of a piece of ground called the Great Orchard. [Photograph courtesy of Audrey Humphrey]

TANNER STREET, 1967

This photograph was taken from the first floor window of the King Street branch of the Midland Bank early in 1967. A few days later the destruction of the buildings that lined Tanner Street began. After the site was cleared, work began constructing the Riverside Walk development. [Photograph courtesy of Rita Christian]

TANNER STREET, 1967

The demolition of maltings and other buildings is well under way. In the centre of this view is the old Tan House which still stands today. The former tannery yard was cleared and opened as a car park in 1961.

Another feature of 19th century Thetford that survived stands almost opposite the Tan House. It is the Methodist Chapel, built by Thetford's Wesleyans in 1830. [Photograph courtesy of Thetford Town Council]

RIVERSIDE WALK, 1995

This part of the Riverside Walk was once the Tanner Street junction with King Street. The Riverside Walk was developed by the Norwich Union Insurance Society and opened in October 1968. Civic representatives from Thetford's twin towns - Boo, Sweden; Hurth, Germany and Spijkenisse, Holland - were present at the official opening ceremony.

The site of Dr Minn's old house is now occupied by Lloyds Bank. [Photograph courtesy of Carl Richards]

THE RIVERSIDE MALTINGS, 1965

At this point, the rivers Thet and Little Ouse meet but apart from the rivers, little else in this view is recognisable today. The maltings and other buildings that lined the river towards the Town Bridge were all demolished in the 1960s to make way for the Riverside Walk development and car parks.

The overgrown piece of land in the left foreground, once known as Buttler's Common, was mistakenly and incorrectly named in the 1970s as Butten Island rather than Buttler's Island. It is now landscaped and since the late 1980s has formed part of an attractive riverside walk. [Photograph courtesy of Thetford Town Council]

RIVERSIDE WALK DEVELOPMENT, 1967

The statue of Thomas Paine [1737-1809], Thetford's celebrated political writer, looks across to the demolition and rebuilding of Thetford. The Red House, that stood opposite the King's House, has just been demolished to provide a service road to the rear of the Riverside Walk development, then in progress.

Paine's gilded statue was unveiled in 1964. It was given to the town by the Thomas Paine Foundation of America. [Photograph courtesy of Thetford Town Council]

THE RIVERSIDE WALK, 1968

This photograph was taken from the Town Bridge just a few weeks before the Riverside Walk was officially opened by the Mayor of Thetford, Councillor B.C. Culey on the 3rd October 1968.

Work on constructing and positioning Butten Bridge had just begun, despite the presence of flood water caused by an exceptionally heavy September rainfall. [Photograph courtesy of Rita Christian]

THETFORD VIEWED FROM THE WEST, 1989

This aerial view, looking down on the Town Bridge spanning the Little Ouse river on a warm summer's day in June 1989, amply illustrates the new Thetford developed in the 1960s and 70s. Gone is the crowded, yet attractive assortment of residential, commercial and industrial buildings that formed the local town or landscape before 1960. With only a few remnants of the old town surviving, a tidier, more formal scene has been created - a result of new trends and planning regulations that were unknown when the earlier Thetford evolved. A most noticeable feature in the town centre today is the amount of space given to the parking of motor cars. Undoubtedly our love affair with the motor car has greatly influenced the appearance of the town.

As we approach a new millennium, it is intriguing to speculate how this view and other parts of the town will change in the future. Considering the dynamic nature of humans and our driving passion for change and progress, we must assume that at some time in the future, for whatever reasons, it will be altered and changed. [Photograph by Derek A. Edwards (courtesy of Norfolk Museum Services), 15 June 1989. Ref: TL8683/ACE/DHS11]